Uncover 1

Combo B
with Digital Pack

Ben Goldstein • Ceri Jones
with Kathryn O'Dell

Student's Book

CAMBRIDGE
UNIVERSITY PRESS

Discovery
EDUCATION

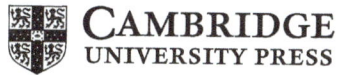

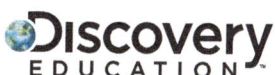

CAMBRIDGE
UNIVERSITY PRESS

University Printing House, Cambridge CB2 8BS, United Kingdom

One Liberty Plaza, 20th Floor, New York, NY 10006, USA

477 Williamstown Road, Port Melbourne, VIC 3207, Australia

314–321, 3rd Floor, Plot 3, Splendor Forum, Jasola District Centre, New Delhi – 110025, India

103 Penang Road, #05–06/07, Visioncrest Commercial, Singapore 238467

Cambridge University Press is part of the University of Cambridge.

It furthers the University's mission by disseminating knowledge in the pursuit of education, learning and research at the highest international levels of excellence.

www.cambridge.org
Information on this title: www.cambridge.org/9781107515017

© Cambridge University Press 2015

This publication is in copyright. Subject to statutory exception and to the provisions of relevant collective licensing agreements, no reproduction of any part may take place without the written permission of Cambridge University Press.

First published 2015

20 19 18 17 16

Printed in Great Britain by CPI Group (UK) Ltd, Croydon CR0 4YY

A catalog record for this publication is available from the British Library

ISBN 978-1-107-51501-7 Combo 1B with Digital Pack

Additional resources for this publication at www.cambridge.org/uncover

Cambridge University Press has no responsibility for the persistence or accuracy of URLs for external or third-party Internet websites referred to in this publication and does not guarantee that any content on such websites is, or will remain, accurate or appropriate. Information regarding prices, travel timetables, and other factual information given in this work is correct at the time of first printing but Cambridge University Press does not guarantee the accuracy of such information thereafter.

Art direction, book design, layout services, and photo research: QBS Learning
Audio production: John Marshall Media

Acknowledgments

Many teachers, coordinators, and educators shared their opinions, their ideas, and their experience to help create *Uncover*. The authors and publisher would like to thank the following people and their schools for their help in shaping the series.

In Mexico:

María Nieves Maldonado Ortiz (Colegio Enrique Rébsamen); Héctor Guzmán Pineda (Liceo Europeo); Alfredo Salas López (Campus Universitario Siglo XXI); Rosalba Millán Martínez (IIPAC [Instituto Torres Quintero A.C.]); Alejandra Rubí Reyes Badillo (ISAS [Instituto San Angel del Sur]); José Enrique Gutiérrez Escalante (Centro Escolar Zama); Gabriela Juárez Hernández (Instituto de Estudios Básicos Amado Nervo); Patricia Morelos Alonso (Instituto Cultural Ingles, S.C.); Martha Patricia Arzate Fernández, (Colegio Valladolid); Teresa González, Eva Marina Sánchez Vega (Colegio Salesiano); María Dolores León Ramírez de Arellano, (Liceo Emperadores Aztecas); Esperanza Medina Cruz (Centro Educativo Francisco Larroyo); Nubia Nelly Martínez García (Salesiano Domingo Savio); Diana Gabriela González Benítez (Colegio Ghandi); Juan Carlos Luna Olmedo (Centro Escolar Zama); Dulce María Pascual Granados (Esc. Juan Palomo Martínez); Roberto González, Fernanda Audirac (Real Life English Center); Rocio Licea (Escuela Fundación Mier y Pesado); Diana Pombo (Great Union Institute); Jacobo Cortés Vázquez (Instituto María P. de Alvarado); Michael John Pryor (Colegio Salesiano Anáhuac Chapalita)

In Brazil:

Renata Condi de Souza (Colégio Rio Branco); Sônia Maria Bernal Leites (Colégio Rio Branco); Élcio Souza (Centro Universitário Anhaguera de São Paulo); Patricia Helena Nero (Private teacher); Célia Elisa Alves de Magalhães (Colégio Cruzeiro-Jacarepaguá); Lilia Beatriz Freitas Gussem (Escola Parque-Gávea); Sandra Maki Kuchiki (Easy Way Idiomas); Lucia Maria Abrão Pereira Lima (Colégio Santa Cruz-São Paulo); Deborah de Castro Ferroz de Lima Pinto (Mundinho Segmento); Clara Vianna Prado (Private teacher); Ligia Maria Fernandes Diniz (Escola Internacional de Alphaville); Penha Aparecida Gaspar Rodrigues (Colégio Salesiano Santa Teresinha); Silvia Castelan (Colégio Santa Catarina de Sena); Marcelo D'Elia (The Kids Club Guarulhos); Malyina Kazue Ono Leal (Colégio Bandeirantes); Nelma de Mattos Santana Alves (Private teacher); Mariana Martins Machado (Britannia Cultural); Lilian Bluvol Vaisman (Curso Oxford); Marcelle Belfort Duarte (Cultura Inglesa-Duque de Caxias); Paulo Dantas (Britannia International English); Anauã Carmo Vilhena (York Language Institute); Michele Amorim Estellita (Lemec – Lassance Modern English Course); Aida Setton (Colégio Uirapuru); Maria Lucia Zaorob (CEL-LEP); Marisa Veiga Lobato (Interlíngua Idiomas); Maria Virgínia Lebrón (Independent consultant); Maria Luiza Carmo (Colégio Guilherme Dumont Villares/CEL-LEP); Lucia Lima (Independent consultant); Malyina Kazue Ono Leal (Colégio Bandeirantes); Debora Schisler (Seven Idiomas); Helena Nagano (Cultura Inglesa); Alessandra de Campos (Alumni); Maria Lúcia Sciamarelli (Colégio Divina Providência); Catarina Kruppa (Cultura Inglesa); Roberto Costa (Freelance teacher/consultant); Patricia McKay Aronis (CEL-LEP); Claudia Beatriz Cavalieri (By the World Idiomas); Sérgio Lima (Vermont English School); Rita Miranda (IBI – [Instituto Batista de Idiomas]); Maria de Fátima Galery (Britain English School); Marlene Almeida (Teacher Trainer Consultant); Flávia Samarane (Colégio Logosófico); Maria Tereza Vianna (Greenwich Schools); Daniele Brauer (Cultura Inglesa/AMS Idiomas); Allessandra Cierno (Colégio Santa Dorotira); Helga Silva Nelken (Greenwich Schools/Colégio Edna Roriz); Regina Marta Bazzoni (Britain English School); Adriano Reis (Greenwich Schools); Vanessa Silva Freire de Andrade (Private teacher); Nilvane Guimarães (Colégio Santo Agostinho)

In Ecuador:

Santiago Proaño (Independent teacher trainer); Tania Abad (UDLA [Universidad de Las Americas]); Rosario Llerena (Colegio Isaac Newton); Paúl Viteri (Colegio Andino); Diego Maldonado (Central University); Verónica Vera (Colegio Tomás Moro); Mónica Sarauz (Colegio San Gabriel); Carolina Flores (Colegio APCH); Boris Cadena, Vinicio Reyes (Colegio Benalcázar); Deigo Ponce (Colegio Gonzaga); Byron Freire (Colegio Nuestra Señora del Rosario)

The authors and publisher would also like to thank the following contributors, script writers, and collaborators for their inspired work in creating *Uncover*:
Anna Whitcher, Janet Gokay, Kathryn O'Dell, Lynne Robertson, and Dana Henricks

Unit	Vocabulary	Grammar	Listening	Conversation (Useful language)
6 Time to Eat! pp. 54–63	■ Food ■ More food ■ Meals	■ *a/an* ■ *some/any* with countable and uncountable nouns ■ *there is/are* ■ *much, many,* and *a lot of* Grammar reference p. 111	■ A conversation about after-school snacks	■ Ordering food
7 Animal World pp. 64–73	■ Animals ■ Action verbs	■ Present continuous ■ Simple present vs. present continuous Grammar reference p. 112	■ Conversations at a zoo	■ Asking for and giving directions
8 City Life pp. 74–83	■ Places in town ■ Transportation places ■ Prepositions of place	■ Simple past of *be* ■ *there was/were* ■ Simple past statements with regular and irregular verbs ■ *ago* Grammar reference p. 113	■ A report on a school trip	■ Sharing exciting news
9 Fun and Games pp. 84–93	■ Sports and activities ■ Clothes	■ Simple past yes/no questions and short answers ■ Simple past Wh- questions Grammar reference p. 114	■ A conversation about a skateboard competition	■ Expressing interest
10 Vacation: Here and There pp. 94–103	■ Weather ■ Months ■ Seasons ■ Landforms	■ *be going to* ■ Superlative adjectives Grammar reference p. 115	■ A conversation about a trip to Ecuador	■ Making suggestions

Unit 6–10 Review Game pp. 104–105

Writing	Reading	Video	Accuracy and fluency	Speaking outcomes
■ An article about a special meal	■ *Art You Can Eat!* ■ Reading to write: *Let's Celebrate!* ■ Culture: *Chino Meets Latino*	■ *Fishing in Japan* ■ *What do you usually have for lunch?* ■ *Dabbawallas* ■ *Mountains of Rice* (CLIL Project p. 118)	■ Linking vowel sounds with *an* ■ Not using *much* in affirmative sentences	I can . . . ■ identify different kinds of food. ■ ask and answer questions about food. ■ talk about quantities of food and meals. ■ order food in a restaurant. ■ talk about food and culture.
■ A description of an animal	■ *Animal Actions Quiz* ■ Reading to write: *All about Hippos* ■ Culture: *Huskies: The Inuit's Best Friend*	■ *Shark Attack!* ■ *Do you like going to museums?* ■ *Animals in the City* ■ *Chameleons* (CLIL Project p. 119)	■ Irregular plural words for animals ■ Different *g* sounds: *going* ■ Verbs usually used in the simple present, not the present continuous	I can . . . ■ identify different animals. ■ ask and answer questions about animals' actions. ■ talk about my favorite zoo animal. ■ ask for and give directions. ■ talk about how animals help people.
■ An email about a place	■ *Pompeii* ■ Reading to write: *My trip to Puebla* ■ Culture: *Getting Around in Hong Kong*	■ *Rome: Ancient and Modern* ■ *Where do you usually go with your friends?* ■ *Crossing Cities*	■ Different sounds for *-ed* endings: /t/, /d/, /ɪd/ ■ Using *were* after singular subjects when they're part of a list	I can . . . ■ talk about places in my city or town. ■ ask and answer questions about the past. ■ describe past events and activities. ■ share exciting news and experiences. ■ talk about transportation and how I get to school.
■ A biography of an athlete	■ *Sumo Giants* ■ Reading to write: *A Teen Athlete* ■ Culture: *Ye Olde English Faire*	■ *The Palio* ■ *What's your favorite sport and why?* ■ *The Bowler*	■ Using some words for sports as both nouns and verbs ■ Reduction of *did you* to /dɪdʒə/ ■ Using *did* (not *do*) in past tense *Wh-* questions	I can . . . ■ identify different sports and activities. ■ ask and answer *yes/no* questions about past events. ■ ask and answer *Wh-* questions about past events. ■ express interest in what someone is saying. ■ talk about traditional sports events.
■ An email about a vacation	■ *Wish You Were Here* ■ Reading to write: *My Trip to Brazil* ■ Culture: *Canada: Land of Surprises*	■ *City of Water* ■ *Where do you like going on vacation?* ■ *Alaska!* ■ *Big Art* (CLIL Project p. 120)	■ Reduction of *going to* to /gənə/ ■ Remembering the apostrophe in *let's*	I can . . . ■ talk about weather, seasons, and months. ■ discuss vacation plans. ■ describe different landforms and places to visit. ■ make suggestions. ■ share interesting facts about my country.

Irregular verbs p. 121

6 Time to Eat!

Discovery EDUCATION
BE CURIOUS

- Fishing in Japan
- What do you usually have for lunch?
- Dabbawallas
- Mountains of Rice

1. What food is in the photo?

2. Do you eat these foods?

3. Why do you think they are in the shape of a heart?

UNIT CONTENTS

Vocabulary Food; more food and meals
Grammar a/an; some/any with countable and uncountable nouns; there is/are with much, many, and a lot of
Listening A conversation about after-school snacks

Vocabulary: Food

1. Write the words next to the correct numbers.

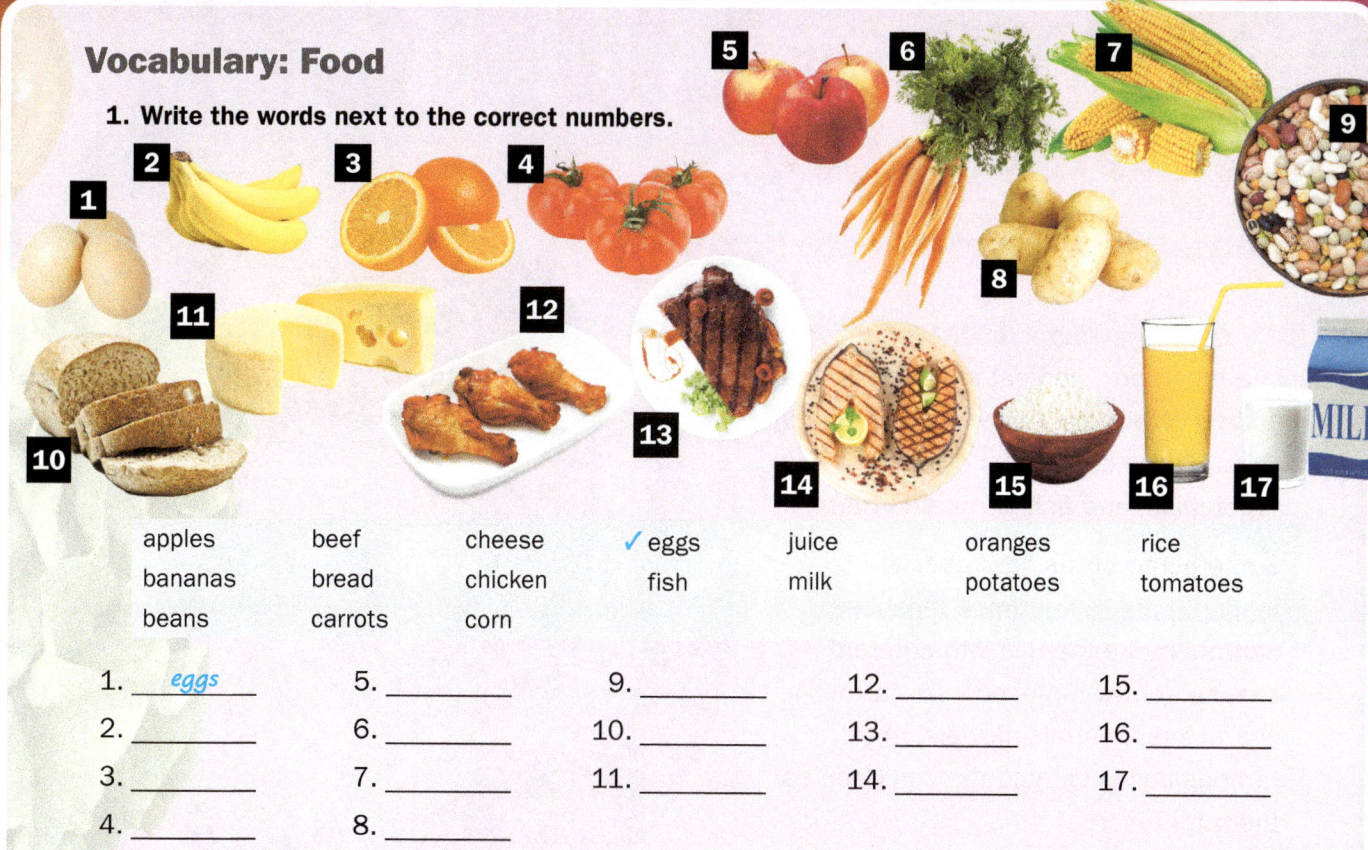

apples	beef	cheese	✓ eggs	juice	oranges	rice
bananas	bread	chicken	fish	milk	potatoes	tomatoes
beans	carrots	corn				

1. _eggs_
2. _____
3. _____
4. _____

5. _____
6. _____
7. _____
8. _____

9. _____
10. _____
11. _____

12. _____
13. _____
14. _____

15. _____
16. _____
17. _____

 2. Listen, check, and repeat.

3. Put the food from Exercise 1 in the correct categories.

Food from animals	Food from plants	
cheese	_apples_	_____
_____	_____	_____
_____	_____	_____
_____	_____	_____
_____	_____	_____
_____	_____	_____

➡ *Spell it* **RIGHT!**
Add **-es** (not **-s**) to **tomato** and **potato** to make them plural.

Speaking: Your likes and dislikes

4. **YOUR TURN** Work with a partner. Ask if your partner likes the food in Exercise 1. Answer with more information.

   Do you like beans?

   Yes, I do. I'm a vegetarian. I eat beans every day! Do you like . . . ?

5. Join another pair. Tell them about the food your partner likes and doesn't like.

   Belinda likes beans, carrots, and oranges. She doesn't like fish or eggs.

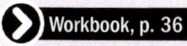 Workbook, p. 36

Reading Art You Can Eat!; Let's Celebrate!; Chino Meets Latino
Conversation Ordering food
Writing An article about a special meal

WHAT'S for LUNCH?
Art You Can Eat!

Do you know what a bento box is? It's a meal in a box. It comes from Japan, and it's great for school lunches! Pack your lunch in a bento box, and eat in style! It's healthy and fun! No more sandwiches and potato chips. These little boxes often have rice, vegetables, and fish or meat in them.

Some bento boxes have special food in them. Sometimes Japanese parents make the rice into different shapes, for example, popular cartoon characters, animals, flowers, and famous buildings! And their children eat them for lunch.

Let's look at Kazuyo's bento box. What does she have for lunch? She says, "I have some rice and some fish, but I don't have any meat today. My rice is in the shape of an animal. I have two pandas! They're really cute!"

a
b
c

Reading: An article about an interesting lunch

1. Look at the photos. What food do you see?

2. Read and listen to the article. Which photo shows Kazuyo's bento box?

3. Read the article again. Answer the questions.

   1. What is a bento box? _____
   2. Where are bento boxes from? _____
   3. Where do children often eat the food in their bento boxes? _____
   4. How is the food sometimes special in a bento box? _____

4. **YOUR TURN** Work with a partner. Are your lunches like Kazuyo's? How are they the same or different?

   > I don't have lunches like Kazuyo's. I buy my lunch at school and usually have meat.

DID YOU KNOW...?
There are more than 40,000 kinds of rice! Japanese people often eat rice at breakfast, lunch, and dinner.

Grammar: *a/an*; *some* and *any* with countable and uncountable nouns

5. Complete the chart.

Use *a/an* or numbers to express quantity with countable nouns. Don't use *a/an* or numbers with uncountable nouns. Use *some* and *any* with both countable and uncountable nouns.

Countable nouns		Uncountable nouns
a panda **an a**nimal	**two** _____ **three** animal**s**	chicken, cheese, corn
Do you have **any vegetables**? Yes, I have **some vegetables**. No, I don't have _____ **vegetables**.		Does she have **any rice**? Yes, she has _____ **rice**. No, she doesn't have **any rice**.

 Check your answers: Grammar reference, p. 111

6. Circle the correct answers.

1. I'm a vegetarian. I don't eat **some** / **any** meat.
2. I eat **a** / **an** orange every day.
3. I'm really thirsty. I need **any** / **some** juice.
4. Jerold has **any** / **some** carrots in his lunch.
5. Do we have **a** / **any** milk?
6. I have **a** / **an** tomato on my sandwich.

7. Complete the paragraphs with *a*, *an*, *some*, or *any*. Then match the paragraphs with the pictures.

"In my basket, I have [1] *some* milk, [2] _____ cheese, and [3] _____ apple. I also have [4] _____ carrots. I don't have [5] _____ fish, but I have [6] _____ chicken."

"In my basket, I have [7] _____ eggs and [8] _____ juice. I don't have [9] _____ carrots, but I have [10] _____ apples and [11] _____ banana. I don't have [12] _____ meat, but I have [13] _____ fish."

a

b

Speaking: What's in your basket?

8. **YOUR TURN** You are at a supermarket. Choose five food items for your shopping basket.

five potatoes, some corn, an apple, some juice, some eggs

9. Work with a partner. Find out what food items are in your partner's shopping basket. Draw them.

> Do you have any bread in your basket?
>> No, I don't.
> Do you have any potatoes?
>> Yes, I do. I have five potatoes.

Say it RIGHT!

We often link **an** with the vowel sound that follows it. Listen and repeat.

an apple   **an e**gg   **an o**range

Link any words that start with a vowel and follow **an** in Exercise 8.

BE CURIOUS Find out about fishing in Japan. What kind of fish is popular in Japan and all over the world? (Workbook p. 82)

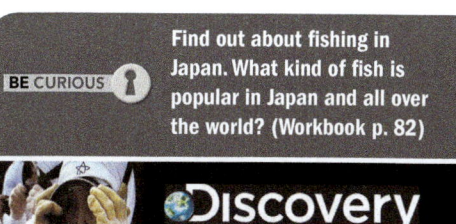

6.1 FISHING IN JAPAN

Workbook, pp. 36–37

Unit 6 | 57

Let's make A SNACK.

Listening: I'm hungry!

1. Do you eat food after school? What do you eat?

2. Listen to Lucia and Ethan. What do they talk about? Who joins their conversation at the end?

3. Listen again. Do they eat or drink these things? Write *Yes* or *No*.

	Lucia	Ethan
1. crackers and cheese		
2. cheese sandwiches		
3. apple juice		
4. water		
5. cake		

Vocabulary: More food and meals

4. Match the words with the pictures. Then listen and check your answers.

1. _f_ a burger
2. ____ a salad
3. ____ a sandwich
4. ____ cake
5. ____ cereal
6. ____ crackers
7. ____ ice cream
8. ____ nuts
9. ____ pasta
10. ____ soup
11. ____ sushi
12. ____ tacos
13. ____ yogurt

5. Match the meals with their definitions.

1. breakfast _d_
2. lunch ____
3. dinner ____
4. dessert ____
5. a snack ____

a. food after dinner, usually sweet
b. food in between meals
c. a meal in the afternoon
d. a meal in the morning
e. a meal in the evening

6. **YOUR TURN** Work with a partner. What do you usually eat for each meal? Use the words from Exercise 4 and your own ideas.

> I usually have cereal and a banana for breakfast. For lunch, I have . . .

Grammar: *there is/are* with *much*, *many*, and *a lot of*

7. Complete the chart.

	Use *there is/are* with *much*, *many*, and *a lot of* to express quantity.
Countable nouns	How many crackers **are there**? **There are** four crackers. **There are a lot of** crackers. = **There are many** crackers. **There aren't a lot of** crackers. = _____ **many** crackers. **Are there any** crackers? Yes, _____. No, there aren't.
Uncountable nouns	How much bread **is there**? **There's a lot of** bread. **There isn't a lot of** bread. = _____ **much** bread. _____ **any** bread? Yes, **there is.** No, _____. But **there is some** rice.
Contractions	**There is** = _____

> Check your answers: Grammar reference, p. 111

8. Complete the questions and answers with the correct form of *there is/are*.

1. **A:** *Are there* _____ any oranges in the kitchen?
   B: Yes, _____. _____ six oranges.
2. **A:** _____ any bread here?
   B: No, _____. But _____ some crackers.
3. **A:** How many eggs _____ in the fridge?
   B: _____ any eggs in the fridge.
4. **A:** How much pasta _____?
   B: _____ a lot of pasta!
5. **A:** _____ any cake left?
   B: Yes, _____. And _____ some ice cream, too!

> **Get it RIGHT!**
> Don't use **much** in affirmative sentences.
> There is **a lot of** soup in my bowl.
> NOT: ~~There is **much** soup in my bowl.~~

9. Complete the questions with *how much* or *how many*. Then look at the picture and write answers with *a lot of*, *much*, or *many*.

1. *How many* nuts are there? *There are a lot of nuts. / There are many nuts.*
2. _____ tacos are there? _____
3. _____ ice cream is there? _____
4. _____ juice is there? _____
5. _____ bananas are there? _____

Speaking: A good recipe

10. YOUR TURN Work with a partner. Talk about meals you like. Ask and answer questions about the ingredients in it.

> I really like my mom's chili.
> Is there any beef in it?
> No, there isn't.
> Are there beans in it?
> Yes, there are a lot of beans in it.

11. Join another pair. Tell the pair about your partner's meal.

> Jackie likes her mom's chili. There isn't any beef in it, but there are a lot of beans in it. There are also . . .

> Workbook, pp. 38–39

Unit 6 | 59

 **REAL TALK** 6.2 WHAT DO YOU USUALLY HAVE FOR LUNCH?

What's COOKING?

Conversation: At a café

 1. **REAL TALK** Watch or listen to the teenagers. Circle the food they talk about.

Chicken	Salad	Vegetables	Fruit
chicken sandwiches	egg salad	carrots	an orange
chicken salad	steak salad	corn	an apple
chicken tacos	Caesar salad	potatoes	a banana
chicken soup	tomato salad	lettuce	tomatoes

2. **YOUR TURN** What do *you* usually have for lunch? Tell your partner.

 3. Listen to Kevin ordering food at a café. Complete the conversation.

USEFUL LANGUAGE: Ordering food
What can I get you?   Can I have   Anything else?   I'd like

Server: Hello. ¹_____
Kevin: Let's see.... ²_____ a sandwich?
Server: Sure. What kind of sandwich do you want?
Kevin: ³_____ a **chicken** sandwich, please.
Server: No problem.
Kevin: Oh, and I'd like some soup, too.
Server: What kind of soup would you like?
Kevin: Um, **potato** soup.
Server: OK. ⁴_____
Kevin: No, I don't think so. Oh, wait! Yes. I also want some juice.
Server: What kind of juice?
Kevin: Sorry! **Apple** juice, please.
Server: OK. That's a **chicken** sandwich, **potato** soup, and **apple** juice.
Kevin: Yes, that's right. Thank you.

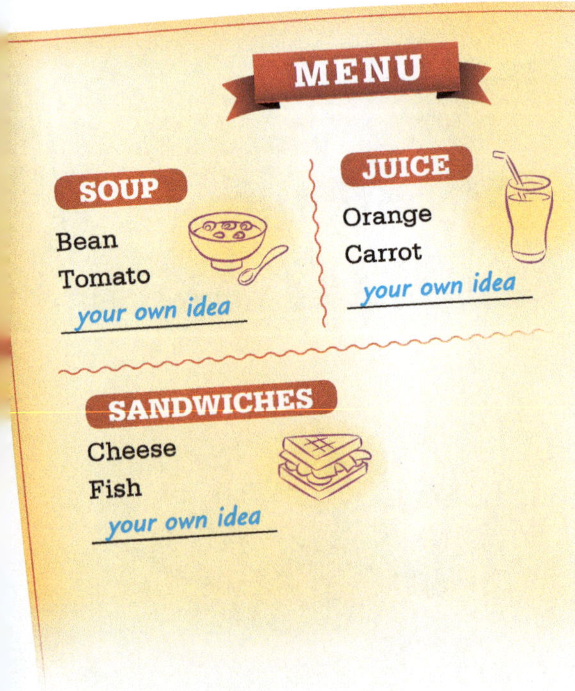

4. Practice the conversation with a partner.

5. **YOUR TURN** Repeat the conversation in Exercise 3, but change the words in purple. Use the information on the menu.

MENU

SOUP
Bean
Tomato
your own idea

JUICE
Orange
Carrot
your own idea

SANDWICHES
Cheese
Fish
your own idea

Let's Celebrate!
by Eva Roma

I celebrate my birthday every June with a big dinner party! It's hot here in June, so we have dinner outside at my grandparents' house. My parents, sister, grandparents, and a lot of my friends come to the party.

Before dinner, my friends and I play games. While we play, my grandma cooks my favorite food—bean soup and chicken tacos. We usually eat at 4:00. After dinner, I open presents. Then we have carrot cake and ice cream for dessert. Dessert is my favorite part! I love my birthday!

Reading to write: Eva's special dinner

6. Look at the photo of Eva. What is the celebration? Read the text to check.

> *Focus on* **CONTENT**
> An article about a special meal can include this information:
> *What* (the event, food, activities)
> *When* (month, time, or day)
> *Where* (place)
> *Who* (people)

7. Read about Eva's special dinner again. Find examples for the categories in the Focus on Content box.

> *Focus on* **LANGUAGE**
> **Time connectors**
> Use the time connectors *before*, *after*, *while*, and *then* to describe the order of events.
> **Before** breakfast, I take a shower.
> **After** breakfast, I brush my teeth.
> **While** I take a shower, I listen to music.
> **Then** I go to school.

8. Find examples of each use of time connectors in Eva's article.

9. Circle the correct time connectors.
1. **While / Before** dinner, I do my homework.
   Then / Before I watch TV.
2. I eat lunch at 12:00 on Saturdays. **After / Before** lunch, at about 1:00, I ride my bike to the park. **While / Then** I'm at the park, I play with my friends.
3. I come home after soccer practice. **After / While** that, I have a snack. **Then / Before** I play games on my laptop.

 **Writing:** A special meal

PLAN
Choose a special event that has a special meal. Write notes about the event and the meal.

What	Where	When	Who

WRITE
Now write about the event. Use your notes to help you. Write at least 80 words.

CHECK
Check your writing. Can you answer "yes" to these questions?

- Is information from the Focus on Content box in your text?
- Are there time connectors in your text?

CHINO meets LATINO!

Los Angeles (LA) is a fast, fun, and diverse city. No wonder fusion food trucks are popular in LA! Fusion food is the combination of two types of food from different cultures. Food trucks serve food from the side of the road. With people from a lot of different cultures and people always in a hurry, LA is the perfect place for fusion food trucks.

Don Chow Tacos is a popular food truck in LA. Dominic Lau and Lawrence Lie own it. They are from traditional Chinese families, but they are near a lot of Mexican food. They put the two types of food together! Ernie Gallegos cooks their recipes. There are a lot of interesting meals at Don Chow Tacos. A favorite meal is the Kung Pau Chicken *chimale*. A *chimale* is a Chinese-Mexican tamale. The outside is from corn, like a Mexican tamale, and the inside has meat with Chinese flavors.

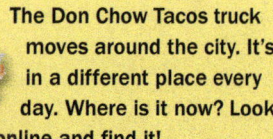

The Don Chow Tacos truck moves around the city. It's in a different place every day. Where is it now? Look online and find it!

Culture: Fusion food trucks

1. Look at the photos. What is the truck for?

2. Read and listen to the article. What kind of food is there at Don Chow Tacos?

3. Read the article again. Answer the questions.
   1. Why are food trucks popular in LA?
   2. What is fusion food?
   3. Who owns Don Chow Tacos? Who cooks?
   4. Where is the food truck each day?
   5. How do people find the food truck?

4. **YOUR TURN** Work with a partner. Create a fusion food and tell your partner about it.

   > My fusion food is curry sushi. There is rice and fish in it like Japanese sushi. There's also curry on it. It's an Indian spice.

DID YOU KNOW...?
There are more than 6,000 food trucks in Los Angeles. Some people follow them around the city.

BE CURIOUS Find out about dabbawallas in Mumbai, India. What does a dabbawalla do? (Workbook, p. 83)

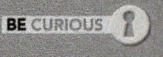

6.3 DABBAWALLAS

UNIT 6 REVIEW

Vocabulary

1. Label the pictures with food and drink words.

1.  _____ and _____

2. _____ and _____

3.  _____ and _____

4. _____ and _____

5.  _____ and _____

6. _____ and _____

2. Complete the paragraph with the correct meals.

I eat ¹_____ at 7:00 in the morning before I go to school. I buy ²_____ at school. We eat at 12:00. When I get home from school, I have a small ³_____. I eat ⁴_____ with my family at 6:30. We have a big meal! After that, we usually have ⁵_____. My favorite is ice cream!

Grammar

3. Complete the sentences with *a*, *an*, *some*, or *any*.

1. I'd like _____ taco, please.
2. Do we have _____ bread?
3. I usually have _____ egg and _____ cereal for breakfast.
4. We don't have _____ cheese, but we have _____ crackers.

4. Circle the correct answers.

1. **There is / There are** nuts on the salad.
2. There isn't **many / much** milk on my cereal.
3. **There isn't / There aren't** any ice cream left.
4. How **many / much** oranges are there?
5. **There is / Is there** any cheese on your sandwich?

Useful language

5. Complete the conversation.

| Anything else? | Can I have | I'd like | What can I get you? |

Server: Hello. Welcome to the Friendly Café. ¹_____

Mike: ²_____ pasta, please.

Server: OK. ³_____

Mike: Yes. ⁴_____ a salad, please?

Server: Sure.

PROGRESS CHECK: Now I can . . .

☐ identify different kinds of food.
☐ ask and answer questions about food.
☐ talk about quantities of food and meals.
☐ order food in a restaurant.
☐ write about a special event and meal.
☐ talk about food and culture.

CLIL PROJECT

6.4 Mountains of Rice, p. 118

7 Animal WORLD

Discovery EDUCATION
BE CURIOUS

Shark Attack!

Do you like going to museums?

Animals in the City

Chameleons

1. Where do polar bears live?

2. What other animals live there?

3. What other animals can swim? What animals can't swim?

UNIT CONTENTS
Vocabulary Animals; action verbs
Grammar Present continuous; simple present vs. present continuous
Listening Conversations at a zoo

Vocabulary: Animals

1. Look at the mixed-up animals. Label each picture with two animals.

- ☐ bird
- ☐ cat
- ☐ cow
- ☐ dog
- ☐ elephant
- ☐ fish
- ☐ frog
- ☐ giraffe
- ☐ gorilla
- ☐ horse
- ☐ monkey
- ☐ pig
- ☑ a polar bear
- ☐ shark
- ☐ sheep
- ☐ spider
- ☑ a tiger
- ☐ zebra

1. _a tiger_ and _a polar bear_
2. _____ and _____
3. _____ and _____
4. _____ and _____
5. _____ and _____
6. _____ and _____
7. _____ and _____
8. _____ and _____
9. _____ and _____

2. Listen, check, and repeat.

3. Work with a partner. Put the animals in Exercise 1 in the correct categories. Some animals can go in more than one category.

Pets	Farm animals	Wild animals	Water animals	Land animals
birds		birds		

Speaking: Create an animal

4. **YOUR TURN** Create an animal like the ones in Exercise 1. Draw a picture of it, and describe it to a partner.

> My animal is part frog and part bird. It's small. It's green and red.

5. Describe your animal to the class.

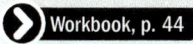
Workbook, p. 44

NOTICE IT
The plural forms of *fish* and *sheep* are irregular.
I have a blue fish. My sister has two yellow fish.
There is one black sheep on the farm and 20 white sheep.

Reading Animal Actions Quiz; All about Hippos; Huskies: The Inuit's Best Friend
Conversation Asking for and giving directions
Writing A description of an animal

Unit 7 | 65

WHAT are the ANIMALS DOING?

ANIMAL ACTIONS QUIZ

Animals are always busy. They do different things for different reasons. Sometimes the reasons aren't what you think they are! How much do you know about animals' actions? Take this quiz and find out!

1 Why is this elephant moving its ears?
a. It's tired.
b. It's hot.
c. It's afraid.

4 What's this frog doing?
a. It's drinking.
b. It's singing.
c. It's eating.

2 What's this horse doing?
a. It's smiling.
b. It's laughing.
c. It's smelling something.

5 What are these monkeys doing?
a. They're playing.
b. They're fighting.
c. They're cleaning each other.

3 What are these giraffes doing?
a. They're fighting.
b. They're dancing.
c. They're playing.

Click on the link to get clues.

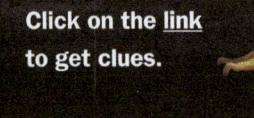

Reading: A quiz about animals

1. Look at the photos in the quiz. What animals do you see?

2. Read and listen to the quiz. Do you know the answers? Circle your guesses. Use the clues to help you.

Clue for #1: Elephants move their ears to stay cool.

Clue for #2: Horses show their teeth when they use their noses.

Clue for #3: When they get angry, giraffes use their long necks to hit each other.

Clue for #4: Male frogs make sounds from a sac under their mouths.

Clue for #5: Monkeys often take bugs and dirt out of each other's fur.

3. Listen and check your answers to the quiz.

4. **YOUR TURN** Work with a partner. What else do you know about the animals in the quiz? What do you know about other animals' actions?

> Elephants' noses are called trunks. Elephants eat and drink with their trunks. They also fight with their trunks.

DID YOU KNOW...?
Frogs live on every continent in the world except Antarctica.

66 | Unit 7

Grammar: Present continuous

5. Complete the chart.

Use the present continuous to talk about activities that are happening now.		
Wh- questions (do)	**Affirmative (play)**	**Negative (dance)**
What **are** you **doing**? What _____ the frog _____? What **are** the monkeys **doing**?	I'**m playing**. It'**s playing**. They _____.	I'**m not dancing**. It _____. They **aren't dancing**.
Yes/No questions (eat)	**Short answers**	
Are you **eating**? **Is** the frog **eating**? _____ the monkeys _____?	Yes, I **am**. Yes, it _____. Yes, they **are**.	No, I'**m not**. No, it **isn't**. No, they _____.

▶ Check your answers: Grammar reference, p. 112

6. Complete the text with the present continuous forms of the verbs.

"Hello, friends! Welcome to Animal World! Where am I? I'm in Vancouver, Canada! And, no, I ¹*'m not talking* (not talk) to you from a swamp! Today, I ² _____ (visit) the Vancouver Aquarium with my sister. Right now, we ³ _____ (listen) to a guide. She ⁴ _____ (talk) to some students about crocodiles. She ⁵ _____ (say) crocodiles are very intelligent. Oh, now the crocodiles ⁶ _____ (jump) in the air! It's lunchtime, and our guide ⁷ _____ (give) them some fish. She ⁸ _____ (not go) very close to them, of course! They ⁹ _____ (show) their big teeth, and they ¹⁰ _____ (eat) a lot of fish at a time!"

7. Write questions (Q) and answers (A) with the present continuous forms of the verbs.

1. **Q:** where / you / go **A:** go / to the zoo
   Q: *Where are you going?*
   A: *I'm going to the zoo.*

2. **Q:** what / the sharks / do **A:** eat / fish
   Q: _____
   A: _____

3. **Q:** Jen / feed / the horses **A:** no
   Q: _____
   A: _____

4. **Q:** the cats / sleep **A:** yes
   Q: _____
   A: _____

5. **Q:** what / bird / doing **A:** sing / a song
   Q: _____
   A: _____

Say it RIGHT! 🔊 7.04

The **g** sound in *-ing* endings is not a hard **g**. Listen and repeat the word. Compare the two **g** sounds.

*go*in*g*

Listen and repeat the questions and answers in Exercise 7. Then practice with a partner.

Speaking: What animal am I?

8. YOUR TURN Work with a partner. Act out an animal. Your partner guesses what you're doing and then guesses the animal. Take turns.

- Are you jumping? — No, I'm not.
- Are you flying? — Yes, I am.
- Are you a bird? — Yes, I am.

BE CURIOUS — Find out about sharks. Where does the Greenland shark live? (Workbook, p. 84)

7.1 SHARK ATTACK

▶ Workbook, pp. 44–45

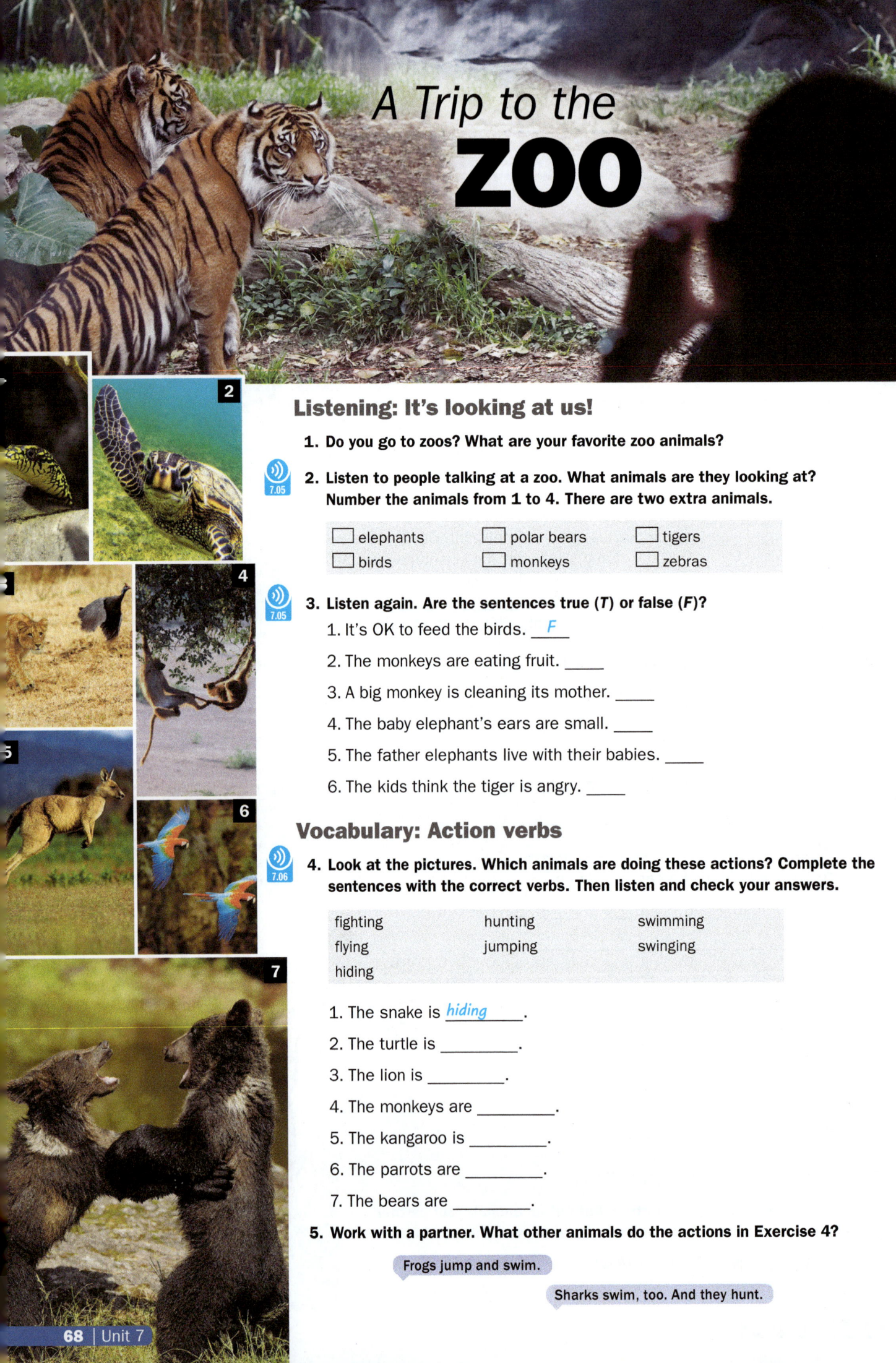

A Trip to the ZOO

Listening: It's looking at us!

1. Do you go to zoos? What are your favorite zoo animals?

2. Listen to people talking at a zoo. What animals are they looking at? Number the animals from 1 to 4. There are two extra animals.

☐ elephants ☐ polar bears ☐ tigers
☐ birds ☐ monkeys ☐ zebras

3. Listen again. Are the sentences true (T) or false (F)?

   1. It's OK to feed the birds. _F_
   2. The monkeys are eating fruit. ____
   3. A big monkey is cleaning its mother. ____
   4. The baby elephant's ears are small. ____
   5. The father elephants live with their babies. ____
   6. The kids think the tiger is angry. ____

Vocabulary: Action verbs

4. Look at the pictures. Which animals are doing these actions? Complete the sentences with the correct verbs. Then listen and check your answers.

fighting	hunting	swimming
flying	jumping	swinging
hiding		

   1. The snake is _hiding_.
   2. The turtle is _____.
   3. The lion is _____.
   4. The monkeys are _____.
   5. The kangaroo is _____.
   6. The parrots are _____.
   7. The bears are _____.

5. Work with a partner. What other animals do the actions in Exercise 4?

   Frogs jump and swim.

   Sharks swim, too. And they hunt.

68 | Unit 7

Grammar: Simple present vs. present continuous

6. Complete the chart.

Use the simple present for facts, habits, and routines.	Use the present continuous to talk about activities that are happening now.
Simple present	**Present continuous**
What **do** monkeys _____? They usually **eat** bananas.	What **is** that monkey **eating**? It _____ a banana at the moment.
Do you _____ to the zoo? Yes, I **do**. I **go** to the zoo once a year.	_____ you **going** to the zoo? Yes, I **am**. I'm _____ to the zoo right now.
Common time expressions	
always, _____, often, sometimes, never once a week, twice a month, every year on Mondays, _____ weekends	now _____ now at the _____

> Check your answers: Grammar reference, p. 112

7. Circle the correct answers.
1. **I never feed** / **I'm never feeding** the animals at the zoo.
2. Look! That snake **hides** / **is hiding** behind a tree.
3. Kangaroos usually **live** / **are living** in groups.
4. **Do you look** / **Are you looking** at the tigers now?
5. The guide **gives** / **is giving** a tour of the aquarium at the moment.
6. Many bears **sleep** / **are sleeping** when it's cold outside.

> **Get it RIGHT!**
> These verbs are usually used in the simple present, not the present continuous.
> **be**   **have** (for possession)
> **love**   **see**   **understand**
> John **has** two cats.
> NOT: ~~John's **having** two cats~~.
> → See more examples in the Grammar reference, p. 112.

8. Complete the ad with the simple present or present continuous forms of the verbs.

RENT-A-PET!

¹ _Do_ you _like_ (like) pets? ² _____ you _____ (live) in a big city or small apartment? It's hard to have pets in some places. Now, you can rent a pet! Sophia Moore ³ _____ (walk) a dog right now. The dog is Lucky. But Lucky ⁴ _____ (not be) Sophia's dog. She ⁵ _____ (rent) Lucky today! She ⁶ _____ (get) the dog on Saturdays and ⁷ _____ (have) him for three hours. She always ⁸ _____ (take) him for walks. Right now, they ⁹ _____ (go) to the park.

Don't wait! Call Rent-A-Pet today!

9. YOUR TURN Work with a partner. What are you doing right now? What do you usually do on Saturdays?

Speaking: At the zoo

10. YOUR TURN Work with a partner. Talk about your favorite zoo animal. Your partner guesses the animal.

> My animal is green and jumps.
> Is it a frog?

11. Now pretend you are at the zoo looking at your favorite animals. Describe their actions to your partner. Your partner draws them.

> One frog is jumping in the water.
> Another frog is eating small fish, and . . .

REAL TALK 7.2 DO YOU LIKE GOING TO MUSEUMS?

At a MUSEUM

Conversation: Asking for and giving directions

1. **REAL TALK** Watch or listen to the teenagers. How many people like each thing? Write the numbers.

Museums	Art museums	History museums	Science museums	Aquariums	Zoos

2. **YOUR TURN** Do *you* like going to museums? Tell your partner.

3. Listen to Shelby asking for directions at a museum. Complete the conversation.

USEFUL LANGUAGE: Asking for and giving directions

It's on | How do I get to | Take | Turn

Shelby: Excuse me. ¹_____ the frog exhibit?
Guide: Oh, that's easy. Walk down this hall.
Shelby: OK.
Guide: ²_____ left at the end of the hall.
Shelby: OK, go straight down the hall, and then left. Then what?
Guide: ³_____ the stairs up to the third floor.
Shelby: OK. Thanks. Is the frog exhibit at the top of the stairs?
Guide: Yes, it is. ⁴_____ the right.
Shelby: Great. Thank you.
Guide: You're welcome.

4. Practice the conversation with a partner.

5. **YOUR TURN** Repeat the conversation in Exercise 3, but change the words in purple. Use the map.

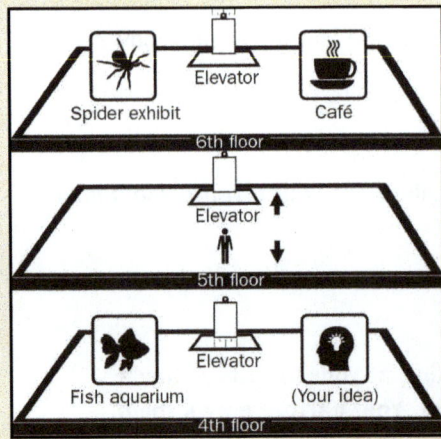
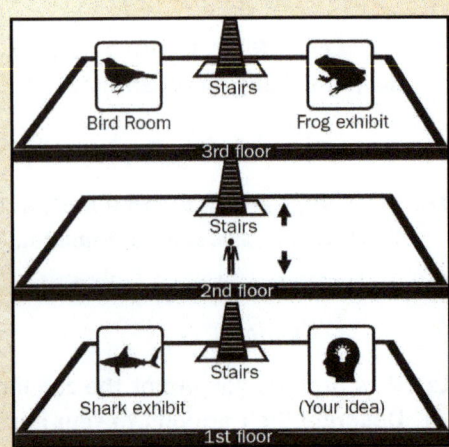

ALL ABOUT HIPPOS

by Sam Wilson

Wild hippopotamuses live in Africa by lakes and rivers. They're big and fat. They have small eyes, small ears, and short legs. They have big mouths and very big teeth! Adult hippos are usually three to four meters long, and they can run very fast!

The hippo in the photo is sleeping in the water. Hippos often sleep in water during the day because the water is cool. It's difficult to see them in the water because they're brown and look like big rocks. Hippos usually come out of the water at night and eat. They only eat plants. They can eat up to 40 kilograms of grass in one night, and they can travel up to 10 kilometers to find food. Hippos can be very dangerous. Every year they kill hundreds of people!

Reading to write: Sam's animal description

6. **Look at the photo. Why is the hippo sleeping in the water? Read the description to check.**

    Focus on **CONTENT**
   A description of an animal can include this information:
   where it lives   its daily activities
   what it looks like   interesting facts about it
   what it eats

   Include a photo and describe what the animal is doing in the photo.

7. **Read the description again. What information did Sam include for each category in the Focus on Content box?**

    Focus on **LANGUAGE**
   Position of adjectives
   Use adjectives:
   - after **is** or **are**: *The gorilla <u>is</u> **big**. Its hands <u>are</u> **big**, too.*
   - before a noun: *A kangaroos has **strong** <u>legs</u>.*
   - after **very**: *Sharks are <u>very</u> **dangerous**.*

8. **Find examples of each use of adjectives in Sam's description.**

9. **Put the words in the correct order to make the sentences.**

   1. cat / I / big / a / have

      I have a big cat.

   2. the tiger / animal / dangerous / is / a

      _____

   3. big / has / ears / the elephant

      _____

   4. are / very / gorillas / strong

      _____

   5. are / and orange / giraffes / brown

      _____

 **Writing:** A description of an animal

○ **PLAN**
Choose an animal. Make a word web with the topics in the Focus on Content box. Find or draw a photo of your animal.

○ **WRITE**
Now write a description of your animal. Use your word web to help you. Write at least 80 words.

○ **CHECK**
Check your writing. Can you answer "yes" to these questions?

- Is information from the Focus on Content box in your profile?
- Are the adjectives in the correct places?

HUSKIES: The Inuit's Best Friend

For many people, dogs are pets. For the Inuit people, dogs are much more than pets. They are an important part of life. Husky dogs help the Inuit in many ways.

The Inuit are the native people of the Arctic. They live in Alaska, Canada, Greenland, and Siberia – places with very cold climates. The Inuit use huskies because the dogs can live in very cold climates, too. The Inuit also use huskies because they are strong and work hard.

Today, many Inuit people live a traditional lifestyle. They use animals for food, transportation, and clothes. In the Arctic, there isn't much fresh fruit, and there aren't many vegetables. In some places, there aren't any supermarkets. So, the Inuit usually eat meat and fish. They hunt seals, polar bears, and reindeer – and their dogs help them do it. When the Inuit look for animals, they travel with their dogs. They make sleds with animal bones and skin, and teams of huskies pull the sleds. The dogs can pull heavy sleds and go very fast.

Huskies are often part of Inuit families. The Inuit love their dogs and can't live without them!

A team of dogs is pulling a sled.

DID YOU KNOW...? A team of huskies with a sled can travel more than 150 kilometers in one day.

Culture: A working animal

1. Look at the title, map, and pictures. Where do the dogs live? What is the weather like?

2. Read and listen to the article. How do huskies help the Inuit? What do the Inuit use other animals for?

3. Read the article again. Are these sentences true (*T*) or false (*F*)? Correct the false sentences.

    1. The Inuit need their huskies. ____
    2. The huskies are strong and fast. ____
    3. The Inuit eat a lot of fruits and vegetables. ____
    4. The Inuit hunt seals, sharks, and reindeer. ____
    5. The huskies can pull heavy sleds. ____

4. **YOUR TURN** Work with a partner. Can you think of any other "working animals"? How do they help people?

    > Some llamas are working animals. They carry things on their backs.

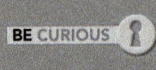 Find out about animals in cities in India. What animals can you see in the cities? (Workbook, p. 85)

7.3 ANIMALS IN THE CITY

UNIT 7 REVIEW

Vocabulary

1. Write sentences about the pictures. Use an animal from box (a) and a verb from box (b).

a	bird	elephant	tiger
	cat	frog	polar bears

b	fight	hide	jump
	fly	hunt	swim

   1. _The tiger is hunting._

   2. _____

   3. _____

   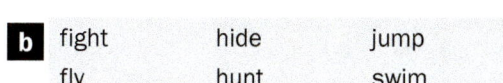
   4. _____

   5. _____

   6. _____

Grammar

2. Write questions in the present continuous.
   1. frog / jump
      _____
   2. what / the birds / do
      _____
   3. where / the cat / hide
      _____
   4. polar bears / hunt
      _____

3. Complete the sentences with the simple present or present continuous forms of the verbs.
   1. Mike _____ (feed) his dog every day.
   2. Anna _____ (read) a book about frogs now.
   3. The bears _____ (not hunt) at the moment.
   4. I usually _____ (not watch) TV shows about animals.

Useful language

4. Complete the conversations.

   | How do I get to | It's on | Take | Turn |

   1. **A:** How do I get to the shark exhibit?
      B: Take the stairs up to the third floor. _____ the right.
   2. **A:** _____ the polar bear exhibit?
      B: Go down this hall. It's on the left.
   3. **A:** Is this the monkey exhibit?
      B: No. Walk down this hall. _____ left by the cafeteria. You can't miss it.
   4. **A:** How do I get to the spider exhibit?
      B: _____ the stairs down to the first floor and go straight.

PROGRESS CHECK: Now I can . . .
- ☐ identify different animals.
- ☐ ask and answer questions about animals' actions.
- ☐ talk about my favorite zoo animal.
- ☐ ask for and give directions.
- ☐ write a description of an animal.
- ☐ talk about how animals help people.

CLIL PROJECT

7.4 Chameleons, p. 119

Vocabulary: Places in town

1. Match the pictures with the words.

1. _f_ a bowling alley
2. ___ a fitness center
3. ___ a mall
4. ___ a market
5. ___ a movie theater
6. ___ a museum
7. ___ a park
8. ___ a skate park
9. ___ a stadium
10. ___ a supermarket

 2. Listen, check, and repeat.

 3. Listen to sounds at different places in town. Write the places from Exercise 1.

1. _a mall_
2. _____
3. _____
4. _____
5. _____
6. _____
7. _____
8. _____
9. _____
10. _____

NOTICE IT
There is food at a **supermarket**, and it is inside a building. Another name for a supermarket is a **grocery store**. There can be food at a **market**, but markets can have other things, too, like clothes. Markets are usually outside.

Speaking: Where do you go?

4. **YOUR TURN** Work with a partner. Ask and answer questions about three places in town from Exercise 1. Take notes on your partner's answers.

Partner's name	Where do you often go in town?	When do you go there?	Who do you go there with?	What do you do there?

> Where do you often go in town?   I often go to the fitness center, the mall, and the movie theater.

5. Join another pair. Tell them about your partner's answers.

> Sergio always goes to the fitness center on the weekends with his best friend. They lift weights and run. He goes to . . .

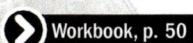 Workbook, p. 50

Reading Pompeii; My trip to Puebla; Getting Around in Hong Kong
Conversation Sharing exciting news
Writing An email about a place

LOST & FOUND

Pompeii: The Lost City

In 79 CE, Pompeii was a large town in Italy with about 20,000 inhabitants. In the evening on August 24, there was a very big volcanic eruption with a lot of ash. After the eruption, there was ash over everything – and everyone – in town. That was the end of Pompeii! Or was it?

Before the eruption, Pompeii was a very busy town with many rich people. There were stores, cafés, schools, and markets. There was also a huge amphitheater – a type of sports stadium. The amphitheater was a very important place. On special days, it was full of people, gladiators, and lions!

How do we know all of this about Pompeii? In 1748, explorers were in Pompeii. The town was still there under the ash! Now the ash isn't there. No one lives in Pompeii today, but many tourists visit the town. It is an outdoor museum. You can see old streets, buildings, and ancient art. You can also see people and animals that were under the ash – frozen in time!

DID YOU KNOW...?
The volcanic eruption in Pompeii was six hours long, covering the town with 15 meters of ash.

Reading: An article about an ancient town

1. Look at the pictures. Where is Pompeii? Can you find these things in the pictures?

| animals | a market | a stadium | a volcano |

 2. Read and listen to the article. What's unusual about Pompeii?

a. There are many volcanoes near the town.

b. No one lives there today because of a volcanic eruption.

c. Many rich people live there.

3. Read the article again. Are these things in Pompeii today or in the past? Write *T* (today) or *P* (past).

1. no people living in Pompeii ____
2. 20,000 people living in Pompeii ____
3. a volcanic eruption ____
4. full of tourists ____
5. busy cafés and markets in town ____
6. gladiators in stadiums ____

4. **YOUR TURN** Work with a partner. Answer the questions.

1. Are there any ancient places or museums with ancient things in your country? Do you go to them?

2. Do you like learning about the past? Why or why not?

> There are ancient Mayan pyramids here.

> And there's a museum with things from the Mayan people.

Grammar: Simple past of *be* and *there was/were*

5. Complete the chart.

Use the simple past of *be* and *there was/were* to describe things in the past.

	Singular	Plural
Simple past of *be*	What **was** Pompeii like? It _____ very busy. It **wasn't** small. _____ Pompeii busy? Yes, it **was**. / No, it _____.	What _____ the people like? They **were** rich. They **weren't** poor. **Were** the people rich? Yes, they _____. / No, they **weren't**.
There was/were	What huge building **was there**? _____ an amphitheater. **There wasn't** a fitness center. **Was there** an amphitheater? Yes, there _____. / No, there **wasn't**.	What kind of buildings **were there**? **There** _____ stores and schools. **There weren't** any airports. **Were there** any stores? Yes, **there were**. / No, **there** _____.

> Check your answers: Grammar reference, p. 113

6. Correct the sentences. Rewrite them with the affirmative and negative forms of the verbs.

1. Palenque was a city in Brazil. (Mexico)

   Palenque wasn't a city in Brazil. It was a city in Mexico.

2. My sisters and I were at the museum. (the skate park)

   _____

3. I was in Italy last week. (last month)

   _____

4. There was a science exhibit at the museum. (a photography exhibit)

   _____
   _____

5. There were 4,000 buildings in Palenque. (1,400 buildings)

   _____
   _____

7. Write questions with the simple past of *be*. Then answer the questions with your own information.

1. where / be / your parents / last night

   Where were your parents last night? They were at home.

2. when / be / you / at the park

   _____

3. what / be / on TV / last night

   _____

Get it RIGHT!

Use **were** (not **was**) with a list of subjects joined by **and** – even if the subject closest to the verb is singular.
*Trucks, cars, and my bicycle **were** on the street.*
NOT: ~~Trucks, cars, and my bicycle **was** on the street.~~

Speaking: Your lost city

8.  Imagine that you and your partner are explorers, and you find a lost, ancient city like Pompeii. Prepare to tell the world about it! Talk about where it was and what it was like. Be creative!

> The city was in Japan. It was a busy city a thousand years ago. There weren't any stores. There were schools, and there was a big market. There weren't any cars, but there were skateboards! There were also . . .

> Workbook, pp. 50–51

BE CURIOUS Find out about Rome, a historic city. What was popular in Rome in the past? (Workbook, p. 86)

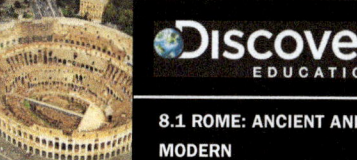

8.1 ROME: ANCIENT AND MODERN

GOING Places

Listening: A trip to an island

1. Where was your most interesting vacation? What was the city or town like?

2. Listen to Leo talk to his class. What is he talking about?
   a. staying in hotels in Peru
   b. his visits to many markets in Peru
   c. his trip to a city and an island in Peru

3. Listen again. Number the events in order.
   ____ He was at a market.   _1_ Leo was in Puno.
   ____ He was in a taxi.   ____ He was at a family's house.
   ____ He was on a boat.   ____ He was in a museum.
   ____ He was on a boat again.   ____ He was on Taquile Island.

Vocabulary: Transportation places and prepositions of place

4. Match the words with the pictures. Then listen and check your answers.
   1. _b_ a bus station   5. ____ a subway station
   2. ____ a bus stop   6. ____ a taxi stand
   3. ____ a ferry port   7. ____ a train station
   4. ____ a parking lot   8. ____ an airport

5. Match the sentences with the pictures. Then listen and check your answers.

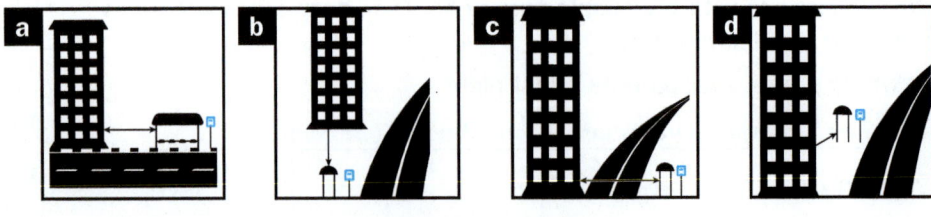

   1. ____ The bus stop is **across from** the building.
   2. ____ The bus stop is **behind** the building.
   3. ____ The bus stop is **next to** the building.
   4. ____ The bus stop is **in front of** the building.

6. **YOUR TURN** Work with a partner. Talk about transportation places in your city or town. Where are they?

   > There is a train station next to a museum in the center of town. There's a bus stop in front my house. There's . . .

Grammar: Simple past statements with regular and irregular verbs

7. Complete the chart.

	Affirmative	Negative
Regular	I **stayed** with a family. You **studied** Spanish. Sarah _____ the hat. They **shopped** at the market.	I _____ in a hotel. You **didn't study** Quechua. She **didn't like** the game. They **didn't shop** at the mall.
Irregular	I **bought** a hat. You _____ to Peru. We **took** buses and taxis.	I **didn't buy** a blanket. You **didn't go** to Chile. We _____ the subway.

Contraction did not = _____

Spell it RIGHT!

For regular verbs:
+ **ed**: show → show**ed**
+ **d**: live → live**d**
-**y** → **i** + **ed**: try → tr**ied**
double consonant + ed: stop → stop**ped**
For irregular verbs: See page 121.

> Check your answers: Grammar reference, p. 113

8. Complete the sentences with the simple past forms of the verbs. The verbs in blue are irregular. Check the correct forms of these verbs on page 121.

I ¹_____ (go) to Egypt last year with my parents and my brother. We ²_____ (fly) to Cairo. We ³_____ (wait) at the airport for a long time! We ⁴_____ (visit) my aunt and uncle. My brother and I ⁵_____ (play) with my cousins. We also ⁶_____ (see) a lot of interesting things. My brother ⁷_____ (like) the pyramids a lot. My cousins live across from a market, and it was my favorite place in Cairo. I ⁸_____ (shop) a lot, but I ⁹_____ (not buy) anything! I ¹⁰_____ (study) Arabic before the trip, so I ¹¹_____ (speak) a little Arabic at the market! But my Arabic wasn't very good. The vendors ¹²_____ (not understand) me!

Say it RIGHT!

Listen to the different sounds of **-ed** endings. Then listen to Exercise 8. Add an example of each sound.

/t/	/d/	/ɪd/
liked	played	waited
_____	_____	_____

9. Write sentences in the simple past with *ago*.

1. the train / arrive / five minutes
   The train arrived five minutes ago.

2. Ephesus / be / a port city / 2,000 years
   _____

3. I / not live / in a big city / three years
   _____

4. We / get / to the airport / an hour
   _____

5. The bus / leave / the station / two minutes
   _____

ago

Use *ago* to say how far back in the past something happened or was.

I went to Peru a month **ago**. There was art from hundreds of years **ago**.

Speaking: Your weekend

10. YOUR TURN Work with a partner. Talk about an interesting trip you took in your town or in another town. Include these things:

- the place(s) you went
- how long ago it was
- the transportation you took
- the activities you did there

> I went to a museum two weeks ago. I took a bus from a bus stop near my house. I saw . . .

11. Join another pair. Tell them about your partner's trip.

> Carrie went to a museum two weeks ago. She took a bus . . .

Workbook, pp. 52–53

REAL TALK 8.2 WHERE DO YOU USUALLY GO WITH YOUR FRIENDS?

It's a GREAT CITY!

Conversation: That sounds fun!

1. **REAL TALK** Watch or listen to the teenagers. Check (✓) the places they go.

   ☐ the bowling alley ☐ the ice cream shop ☐ a museum
   ☐ the fitness center ☐ the mall ☐ the park
   ☐ a café ☐ the market ☐ the shopping center
   ☐ friends' houses ☐ the movie theater ☐ the zoo

NOTICE IT
Some words are different in American and British English.
American | British
mall | shopping centre (center)

2. **YOUR TURN** Where do *you* usually go with your friends? Tell your partner.

3. Listen to David telling Charlie about his weekend. Complete the conversation.

USEFUL LANGUAGE: Sharing exciting news
And that's not all! | Can you believe it? | Did you know that | Guess what!

Charlie: How was your weekend, David?
David: It was great! I went to New York City with my family. We went to the Bronx Zoo and Central Park.
Charlie: That sounds fun!
David: Yeah. ¹_____
Charlie: What else?
David: Well, I did something really fun. ²_____
Charlie: I don't know. What?
David: I went on a helicopter ride! ³_____
Charlie: No, that's so cool!
David: I saw the city from the sky. It's so big! ⁴_____ over 8 million people live there?
Charlie: Wow! That's a lot of people.

4. Practice the conversation with a partner.

5. **YOUR TURN** Repeat the conversation in Exercise 3, but change the words in purple. Use the information in the chart.

City	Places	Population
Rio de Janeiro	Copacabana Beach and Sugar Loaf Mountain	over 6 million
Istanbul	the Galata Tower and the Istanbul Aquarium	over 13 million
London	the British Museum and Buckingham Palace	over 8 million
_____ (your own idea)	_____	_____

80 | Unit 8

Subject: My trip to Puebla

Hi Cindy,

How was your vacation? My trip to Puebla was amazing! Puebla is in the middle of Mexico, and it's very big. Over five million people live there! There are two volcanoes near Puebla, and you can see them from the city.

Puebla is a beautiful city, and it's also very old. We went to the Cholula pyramid. Did you know that the Olmec people built it over 2,000 years ago?

Puebla is a great city for food and art. We went to the Parian. It's a huge market with Mexican arts and crafts. One day, we ate at the Cholula food market. I had chicken with mole poblano. Mole poblano is a sauce with chocolate and chilies. It started in Puebla. We went to the National Museum of Mexican Railways, too. It's a cool train museum!

I can't wait to hear about your vacation!

Your friend,

Isabel

Reading to write: Isabel's email about Puebla

6. Look at the photo. What's Puebla like? Read the email to check.

   ◉ *Focus on* **CONTENT**
   When you write about a place you visited, include this information:
   location   size   history   interesting facts   activities

7. Read the email again. Which paragraphs (1, 2, 3) have information about the categories in the Focus on Content box?

   ◉ *Focus on* **LANGUAGE**
   also and **too**
   Use **also** and **too** to add more information.
   - **Also** goes after the verb **be**: *Tokyo **is** big. It**'s** also busy.*
   - Also goes before other main verbs: *Isabel **loves** chocolate. She **also loves** chilies.*
   - **Too** goes at the end of a sentence: *We went to Rio. We went to São Paulo, **too**.*

8. Find examples of *also* and *too* in Isabel's email.

9. Write sentences with the additional information.

   1. There's a sports stadium in my town. (skate park / also)

      There's also a skate park in my town.

   2. We can go to the mall. (bowling alley / too)

      _____

   3. John bought a hat at the market. (T-shirt / also)

      _____

   4. Seoul is a busy city. (modern / too)

      _____

Writing: An email about a place

○ **PLAN**
Make notes in the chart about a city or town that you visited.

Name of city or town and location	
Size	
History	
Interesting facts	
Activities	

○ **WRITE**
Now write an email to a friend about the place you visited. Use your notes to help you. Write at least 80 words.

○ **CHECK**
Check your writing. Can you answer "yes" to these questions?

- Is information from the Focus on Content box in your profile?
- Do you use *also* and *too* to add more information?

Getting Around in HONG KONG

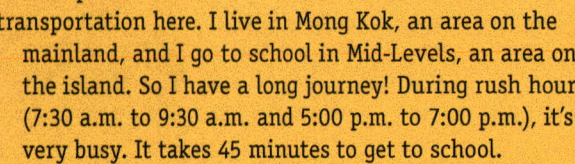

Today, we're looking at interesting and unusual ways to get to school. Twelve-year-old David Wong tells us about his journey to school in Hong Kong.

Part of Hong Kong is on the mainland, and part of it is on an island, so there are many different kinds of public transportation here. I live in Mong Kok, an area on the mainland, and I go to school in Mid-Levels, an area on the island. So I have a long journey! During rush hour (7:30 a.m. to 9:30 a.m. and 5:00 p.m. to 7:00 p.m.), it's very busy. It takes 45 minutes to get to school.

Yesterday was a normal school day. I walked from my apartment to the subway station in Mong Kok. I took the subway to the ferry port, and then I took the ferry across Victoria Harbour.

I arrived on the island, and then I took the tram. I sat on top because you get great views of the city! Finally, I took the escalator to Mid-Levels. Some students go by bus, but I think the escalator is fun!

Culture: Public transportation

1. Look at the title and the photos. What is the article about?

2. Read and listen to the article. Check (✓) the ways David got to school yesterday.

   ☐ walked   ☐ took a train
   ☐ took a tram   ☐ took a ferry
   ☐ took a bus   ☐ took an escalator
   ☐ took a subway   ☐ rode a bike

3. Read the article again. Are the sentences true or false? Write *T* (true), *F* (false), or *NI* (no information).

   1. There are a lot of ways to get around in Hong Kong. ____
   2. Rush hour is in the morning and in the evening. ____
   3. It takes David over an hour to get to school. ____
   4. David has a short walk to the subway station. ____
   5. David sat on the bottom of the tram. ____
   6. David never takes the bus to school. ____

4. **YOUR TURN** Work with a partner. How did you get to school yesterday? How long did it take?

   > Yesterday, I walked to the bus stop and took a bus to school. It took . . .

DID YOU KNOW...?
The escalator system in Hong Kong is on the street. It's 800 meters long and goes up 135 meters. There are 20 escalators in the system.

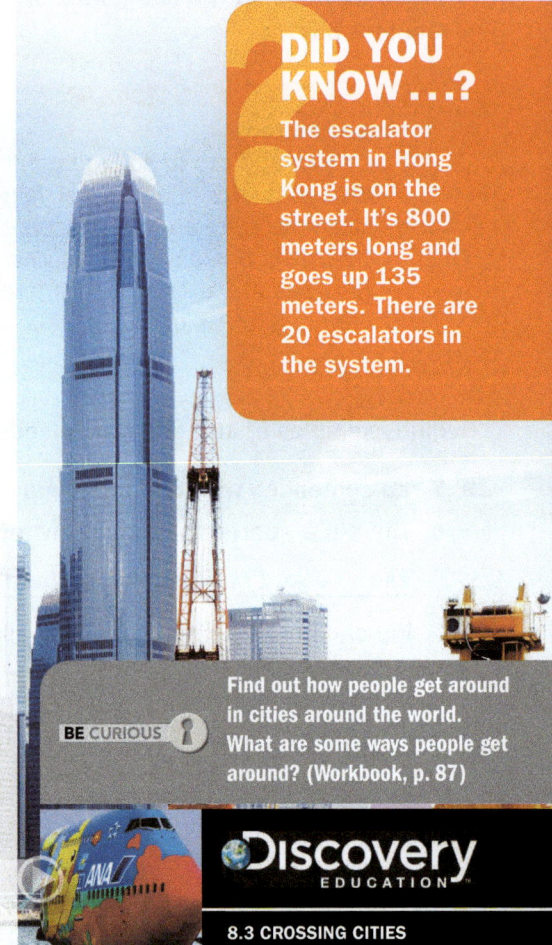

BE CURIOUS Find out how people get around in cities around the world. What are some ways people get around? (Workbook, p. 87)

Discovery EDUCATION
8.3 CROSSING CITIES

UNIT 8 REVIEW

Vocabulary

1. **Where are the people? Match the sentences with the places.**

   a. a supermarket
   b. a fitness center
   c. an airport
   d. a ferry port
   e. a taxi stand
   f. a stadium

   1. ____ I flew to Chicago.
   2. ____ We watched a soccer game.
   3. ____ Emma played basketball with her friends.
   4. ____ I waited for a car for 10 minutes.
   5. ____ My mom bought food for the week.
   6. ____ Luke got on a boat at 9:00 a.m.

2. **Look at the map. Complete the sentences with the correct prepositions of place.**

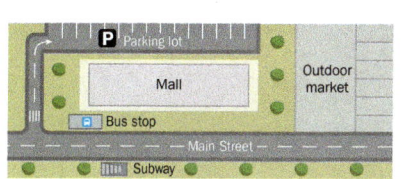

   1. The bus stop is _____ the mall.
   2. The parking lot is _____ the mall.
   3. The subway stop is _____ the mall.
   4. The market is _____ the mall.

Grammar

3. **Complete the questions and answers with *was* or *were*.**

   1. **A:** _____ Sarah at school yesterday?
      B: Yes, she _____.
   2. **A:** _____ you home last night?
      B: No, we _____. We _____ at the movie theater.
   3. **A:** Where _____ Mike in July?
      B: He _____ in Seoul.
   4. **A:** _____ there a volcanic eruption in Quito last week?
      B: No, there _____.
   5. **A:** _____ there places to eat in Pompeii 2,000 years ago?
      B: Yes, there _____. There _____ a lot of outdoor cafés.

4. **Complete the sentences with the simple past forms of the verbs.**

   1. Carol _____ (not go) to the skate park yesterday. She _____ (stay) home and _____ (watch) TV.
   2. Pete _____ (fly) to San José from the Houston airport. Then he _____ (take) a bus to the beach.
   3. Martin _____ (visit) his grandparents in Paris a week ago. He _____ (study) French before the trip.
   4. The bus _____ (not arrive) on time. I _____ (wait) for a long time.
   5. Don and Maria _____ (shop) at the mall for two hours, but they _____ (not buy) anything.

Useful language

5. **Circle the correct answers.**

   1. **A:** I did something really cool this weekend. **And that's not all! / Guess what!**
      B: What?
      A: I went to a new skate park with my cousin.
   2. **A:** My sister got a job in Singapore. **Can you believe it? / And that's not all!**
      B: Wow. That's great!
   3. **A: Did you know that / Guess what** Taquile Island is on a lake between Peru and Bolivia?
      B: No, I didn't. That's interesting.
   4. **A:** How was your weekend?
      B: Great. I went to a museum. **Can you believe it? / And that's not all!** I also went to a movie.

PROGRESS CHECK: Now I can . . .

☐ talk about places in my city or town.
☐ ask and answer questions about the past.
☐ describe past events and activities.
☐ share exciting news and experiences.
☐ write an email about a place.
☐ talk about transportation and how I get to school.

9 Fun and Games

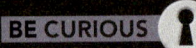
BE CURIOUS

The Palio

What's your favorite sport and why?

The Bowler

1. What is the person doing?
2. Do you know anyone who does this sport?
3. What other exciting sports do you know?

UNIT CONTENTS
Vocabulary Sports and activities; clothes
Grammar Simple past *yes/no* questions and short answers; simple past *Wh-* questions
Listening A conversation about a skateboard competition

Vocabulary: Sports and activities

1. Look at the pictures. Write the phrases next to the correct numbers.

do judo　　　　　go skiing　　　　　play baseball　　　　go windsurfing
go bowling　　　　go snowboarding　　✓ play basketball　　go skateboarding
go cycling　　　　go surfing　　　　　play volleyball

1. _play basketball_　　5. _____　　9. _____
2. _____　　6. _____　　10. _____
3. _____　　7. _____　　11. _____
4. _____　　8. _____

2. Listen, check, and repeat.

3. Look again at the sports and activities in Exercise 1. Which ones . . .

1. are water sports?
2. are sports with a ball?
3. need something with wheels?
4. need a board?
5. are team sports?
6. are individual sports?

NOTICE IT
For sporting activities with **go**, you can also use the name of the sport as a verb.
I go **bowling** on Tuesdays.
OR I **bowl** on Tuesdays.
go cycling → **cycle**
go snowboarding → **snowboard**
You usually cannot do this for sporting activities with **do** or **play**.
She plays **basketball** in the park.
NOT: She basketballs in the park.

Speaking: How active are you?

4. YOUR TURN Work with a partner. Ask and answer the questions.

1. What sports and activities do you do?
2. Where do you do them?
3. How often do you do them?
4. Who do you do them with?

> What sports and activities do you do?
>> I play basketball. I also ski.

5. Join another pair. Tell them about the sports and activities your partner does.

> Lara skis. She goes skiing in the mountains in the winter. She . . .

▶ Workbook, p. 58

Reading Sumo Giants; A Teen Athlete; Ye Olde English Faire
Conversation Expressing interest
Writing A biography of an athlete

SPORTS EVENTS

Sumo Giants

What do you want to know about sumo wrestling? Here's a list of the common questions we receive from readers like you. Check out our responses. If you don't see your question, write to us!

Frequently Asked Questions (FAQs)

1. Did the sport start in China?
2. Is professional sumo wrestling an old or new sport?
3. How many professional wrestlers are there in Japan?
4. Can women wrestle?
5. Do children do sumo wrestling?
6. How much do the wrestlers weigh?
7. How many times a day do they eat?
8. What do they eat?

Answers

a. It's an old sport. It started in the 17th century.
b. They usually eat *chankonabe*, a traditional dish with chicken, fish, beef, tofu, and a lot of vegetables. They also eat a lot of rice.
c. No, they can't. Only men can be professional sumo wrestlers.
d. Yes, they do. You can be a professional wrestler from the age of 15. But sumo isn't very popular with children in Japan today. Japanese children prefer soccer, judo, and baseball.
e. They usually weigh between 120 and 150 kilograms. They are very big men!
f. They typically eat twice a day. Sumo wrestlers don't eat breakfast and often sleep after lunch.
g. No, sumo didn't start in China. It comes from very old Japanese traditions.
h. There are about 700. Not all of the wrestlers are from Japan. There are wrestlers from Hawaii, Mongolia, Bulgaria, Russia, and other countries.

DID YOU KNOW...?
A typical 13-year-old needs about 2,000 to 2,500 calories a day. A sumo wrestler eats about 20,000 calories a day!

Reading: FAQs about sumo wrestlers

1. Work with a partner. Cover the answers to the FAQs. Then read the questions (1–8). Do you know any of the answers?

2. Now read the answers. Match the questions (1–8) with the correct answers (a–h). Then listen and check your answers.

3. Read the questions and answers again. Are these sentences true (*T*) or false (*F*)? Correct the false sentences.

   1. Sumo wrestlers eat three meals a day. ____
   2. There aren't any professional women sumo wrestlers. ____
   3. Japanese children today love sumo wrestling. ____
   4. Sumo wrestlers don't sleep during the day. ____
   5. Sumo wrestling isn't from China. ____
   6. All sumo wrestlers are from Japan. ____

4. **YOUR TURN** Work with a partner. Answer the questions.

   1. What do you think about sumo wrestling? And why?
   2. What sports are traditional in your country? What sports are popular?

   > I think sumo wrestling is cool! It looks like a lot of fun.

   > Maybe, but I don't like it because women can't do it.

Grammar: Simple past yes/no questions and short answers

5. Complete the chart.

> Use simple past yes/no questions to find out if events or activities happened in the past or not.

Yes/No questions	Short answers	
Did you **go** to the game last night?	Yes, I _____.	No, I **didn't**.
_____ Larry **go** to the game last night?	Yes, he **did**.	No, he _____.
Did they _____ to the game last night?	Yes, they _____.	No, they **didn't**.

> Check your answers: Grammar reference, p. 114

6. Complete the conversation with the simple past forms of the verbs.

- **Jane:** ¹ _Did you go_ (you / go) to the baseball game last night?
- **Scott:** Yes, I ² ___did___.
- **Jane:** ³ _____ (you / sit) with your friends?
- **Scott:** No, I ⁴ _____. I sat with my parents.
- **Jane:** ⁵ _____ (you / have) a good time?
- **Scott:** Yes, we ⁶ _____.
- **Jane:** ⁷ _____ (your team / win)?
- **Scott:** No, they ⁸ _____. They lost.
- **Jane:** ⁹ _____ (you / eat) after the game?
- **Scott:** Yes, we ¹⁰ _____. We went to a Chinese restaurant.
- **Jane:** ¹¹ _____ (your parents / like) the food?
- **Scott:** Yes, they ¹² _____.

7. Write yes/no questions with the simple past forms of the verbs.

1. you / go / to a game / last week _Did you go to a game last week?_
2. you / study / last night _____
3. you / play / sports last year _____
4. your friends / play / sports last year _____
5. it / rain / yesterday _____

Say it RIGHT!
9.03
We often reduce **did you** in questions. The words sound like /dɪdʒə/. Listen and repeat the questions in Exercise 7.
Did you go to a game last week? /dɪdʒə/
Ask and answer the questions in Exercise 7 with a partner. Reduce **did you** to /dɪdʒə/.

Speaking: Find someone who . . .

8. **YOUR TURN** Find two people in your class who can answer "yes" to each question. Complete the chart.

Did you . . . last weekend?	Name 1: _____	Name 2: _____
play a sport with a ball		
do a water sport		
go to a sports event		
play a game with friends		

Did you play a sport with a ball last weekend?

Yes, I did. I played volleyball.

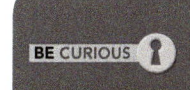

BE CURIOUS Find out about a traditional sports event in Italy. What animals race in the sport? (Workbook, p. 88)

Discovery EDUCATION
9.1 THE PALIO

WHERE did you GO?

Listening: A skateboard competition

1. Do you like going to sports events? Which ones do you like going to?

2. Listen to Vicky telling Joe about a skateboarding competition. Was Vicky in the competition? Did she enjoy it?

3. Listen again. Check (✓) the things that Vicky did.

   ☐ watched her friend skateboard ☐ bought something for Joe
   ☐ jumped with a skateboard ☐ went to lunch with Dennis
   ☐ bought some clothes ☐ ate tacos

Vocabulary: Clothes

4. Match the words with the pictures. Then listen and check your answers.

   1. _c_ a cap
   2. ____ a hoodie
   3. ____ a jacket
   4. ____ a skirt
   5. ____ a sweatshirt
   6. ____ a T-shirt
   7. ____ a tracksuit
   8. ____ boots
   9. ____ jeans
   10. ____ pants
   11. ____ shorts
   12. ____ socks

5. Work with a partner. What clothes do people wear for these sports and activities?

   | baseball | hiking | skateboarding | soccer |

   People wear T-shirts and pants or jeans for hiking.

   They also wear boots, and they sometimes wear jackets.

Grammar: Simple past Wh- questions

6. Complete the chart.

> Use simple past Wh- questions to ask for information about past events and activities.
>
> | | |
> |---|---|
> | _____ did you do? | I went to a skateboard competition. |
> | Who _____ Vicky watch? | Her friend Dennis. |
> | How did Barry get to the game? | By bus. |
> | When _____ it rain? | After the game. |
> | Where did they _____? | To a Mexican restaurant. |
> | _____ many points did our team score? | 20! |

> Check your answers: Grammar reference, p. 114

7. Correct the mistakes.

1. What ~~do~~ *did* you wear to the game yesterday?
2. When did Rick buys that hoodie?
3. Who did Sarah played volleyball with?
4. When does the game end last night?
5. How many goals did we scored?
6. Who do they go surfing with last Saturday?

> **Get it RIGHT!**
> Use **did** (not **do**) with questions in the simple past.
> What **did** you do last night?
> NOT: ~~What **do** you do last night?~~

8. Complete the questions. Use the answers to help you. Then practice with a partner.

Adam: Hey, Terry. Nice cap! ¹*Where did you buy* _____ it?
Terry: I bought it at the game yesterday. The Sharks are my favorite team.
Adam: Cool! ² _____?
Terry: They played the Dragons.
Adam: ³ _____?
Terry: They played at the stadium here in town. It was a great game!
Adam: ⁴ _____?
Terry: They scored four goals. We were so excited!
Adam: We? ⁵ _____ with?
Terry: I went with my friend Kevin.
Adam: Oh. Hey, next time, maybe I can go with you.
Terry: Sure!

Speaking: At the game

9. YOUR TURN Work with a partner. Talk about an interesting sports event or activity from the past. Ask and answer the questions.

1. Where did you go?
2. When did you go?
3. Who did you go with?
4. How did you get there?
5. What did you wear?

> Where did you go?
>
> I went to a baseball game.

10. Join another pair. Tell the pair about your partner's event.

> Claudia went to a baseball game last month. She went with her cousins. They...

Workbook, pp. 60–61

REAL TALK 9.2 WHAT'S YOUR FAVORITE SPORT AND WHY?

FAVORITES and FIRSTS

NOTICE IT
Some words are different in American and British English.

American English	British English
soccer	football
football	American football

Conversation: It sounds fantastic!

1. **REAL TALK** Watch or listen to the teenagers. Check (✓) the sports they talk about.

   ☐ baseball ☐ soccer ☐ snowboarding
   ☐ basketball ☐ swimming ☐ volleyball
   ☐ bowling ☐ table tennis ☐ windsurfing
   ☐ cycling ☐ tennis ☐ wrestling
   ☐ football

2. **YOUR TURN** What's *your* favorite sport and why? Tell your partner.

3. Listen to Rachel telling Max about a windsurfing trip. Complete the conversation.

USEFUL LANGUAGE: Expressing interest
Cool! How was it? Really? What happened?

Max: What did you do this weekend, **Rachel**?
Rachel: I went **windsurfing** for the first time.
Max: Wow! ¹_____
Rachel: It was amazing! But I had problems at first.
Max: Why? ²_____
Rachel: I **fell off the board** a lot!
Max: ³_____ I'm sorry.
Rachel: It's OK. After a few tries, I learned how to do it. I loved it.
Max: ⁴_____ It sounds fantastic!
Rachel: It was!

4. Practice the conversation with a partner.

5. **YOUR TURN** Repeat the conversation in Exercise 3, but change the words in purple. Use the information in the chart.

Sport	Problem
bowling	dropped the ball
inline skating	fell down
surfing	fell off the board
_____ (your own idea)	_____

90 | Unit 9

A TEEN ATHLETE

Mohammed Aman was born in Asella, Ethiopia, on January 10, 1994. At the age of 12, he ran at school and was very fast. In 2008, he won his first international race in Nigeria. He won a silver medal at the World Youth Championship in France in 2011 for the 800-meter race. In that race, he set a national record. He broke his own record in September that same year. On August 9, he came in 6th at the 2012 Olympics in London. At the age of 19, Mohammed won the gold medal at the 2013 World Championships in Moscow. Mohammed wants to go to the next Olympics. He has a great future!

NOTICE IT
- **set a record** = get the best score or time in a sports event
*In 1995, John **set a record** at his school for the most goals in a soccer game.*
- **break a record** = get a better score or time than someone who already had the best
*In 2014, Riana scored more goals and **broke** John's **record**.*

Reading to write: Mohammed's biography

6. Look at the photo. What sport does Mohammed Aman do? Read the biography to check.

Focus on CONTENT
A biography about an athlete can include this information:
- place and year of birth
- sport(s)
- teams and clubs
- medals and records
- his/her future

7. Read the biography again. What happened at these points in Mohammed's life?
- 2008
- August 9, 2012
- the age of 19
- January 10, 1994
- September 2011

Focus on LANGUAGE
Prepositions of time and place
Use the prepositions:
- **on** with dates: *on March 10*
- **in** with months and years: *in December, in 2014*
- **in** with towns/cities and countries: *in Toronto, in Mexico*
- **at** with sports events and ages: *at the World Cup, at the age of five*

8. Find examples of each use of the prepositions in Mohammed's biography.

9. Complete the sentences with the correct prepositions.

1. The diver Qiu Bo was born _____ Neijiang, China, _____ January 31, 1993.
2. _____ the age of five, Karina Petroni started surfing _____ Panama.
3. Diego Reyes's soccer team won the gold medal _____ the Summer Olympics _____ 2012.
4. Tennis player Victoria Duval was born _____ Florida _____ November 30, 1995, but she lived _____ Haiti until she was eight years old.

Writing: A biography of an athlete

PLAN
Choose a young athlete from your country. Write notes about important events in the athlete's life. Use the timeline and the Focus on Content box to help you.

WRITE
Now write the biography. Use your timeline to help you. Include at least five events.

CHECK
Check your writing. Can you answer "yes" to these questions?

- Is information from the Focus on Content box in your profile? Are the events in the order they happened?
- Do you use the correct prepositions of time and place?

Ye Olde ENGLISH FAIRE

Are you interested in the past?
Find a Renaissance fair near you and explore life in another time!

The Renaissance was from the 1300s to the 1600s in Europe. Renaissance fairs are modern outdoor events about this time in history. There are sports, games, food, plays, and music from the past at the fairs. People usually wear old-fashioned clothes at the fairs, too. Some people even speak like they did during the Renaissance!

Jousting and archery were popular during the Renaissance, and they're very popular at fairs today. During the fairs, actors (not athletes) joust. Many fairgoers watch and see what the sport was like during the Renaissance. Anyone can usually join the archery competition.

Renaissance fairs didn't start very long ago. In 1963, Phyllis and Ron Patterson wanted the children in their after-school program in California to learn about history in a new way. They created a "living history," so the children could experience what life was like during the Renaissance. They called it the Renaissance Pleasure Faire. About 8,000 people went. Today, over 200,000 people go to the Pleasure Faire, and Renaissance fairs are very popular all over the United States.

Modern English	Old English
the	ye
fair	faire
old	olde
Good morning.	Good morrow.
How are you?	How now?
What's your name?	What be thy tide?
Good bye.	Fare thee well.

Culture: Renaissance fairs

1. **Look at the pictures. What are the people wearing? What are they doing?**

2. **Read and listen to the article. Number the main ideas of each paragraph (1–3) in the order they appear in the article.**

    ____ sports at Renaissance fairs

    ____ the first Renaissance fair

    ____ the definition of a Renaissance fair

3. **Read the article again. Answer the questions.**

    1. When was the Renaissance? _____

    2. What two sports are popular at Renaissance fairs today?
       _____

    3. Which sport do actors do at the fair? _____

    4. When did the Pattersons have the first Renaissance fair?
       _____

    5. How many people went to the first Renaissance fair?
       _____

4. **YOUR TURN** Work with a partner. Talk about a traditional sport in your country. What do you know about its history?

    > Cricket is a traditional sport. It started in the 1500s. It . . .

DID YOU KNOW . . . ?
During the Renaissance, people bowled and played soccer.

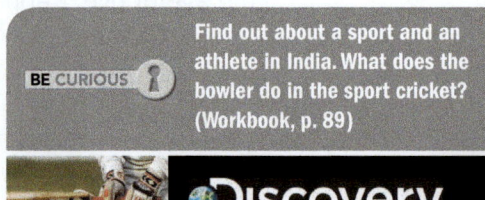

BE CURIOUS
Find out about a sport and an athlete in India. What does the bowler do in the sport cricket?
(Workbook, p. 89)

Discovery EDUCATION
9.3 THE BOWLER

UNIT 9 REVIEW

Vocabulary

1. **Label the pictures with *play*, *do*, or *go* and the correct sport.**

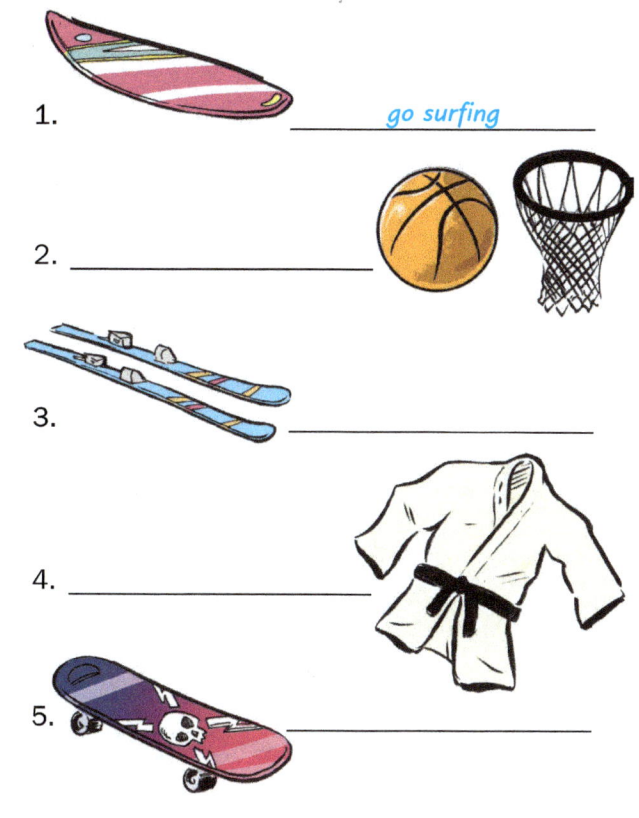

    1. _go surfing_
    2. _____
    3. _____
    4. _____
    5. _____

2. **Circle the correct answers.**

    1. The runner put on thin **socks / shorts / pants** before she put on her sneakers.
    2. The baseball player has a cool **boot / hoodie / cap** on his head.
    3. When it's cold, I wear a **T-shirt / jacket / jeans** over my shirt.
    4. The team's basketball **jeans / skirts / shorts** are blue and orange.
    5. You can't wear shorts to the event. You have to wear a skirt or **pants / boots / cap**.

Grammar

3. **Write *Wh-* or *yes/no* questions with the simple past forms of the verbs.**

    1. you / go / to the game last night
       Did you go to the game last night?
    2. where / Ben / go skateboarding
       _____
    3. who / they / watch / in the race
       _____
    4. the team / get / T-shirts last week
       _____
    5. how many / medals / Kate / win last year
       _____
    6. Pam and Matt / watch / the game on TV
       _____

Useful language

4. **Circle the correct answers.**

    1. **A:** I went skiing for the first time yesterday.
       B: Cool! / What happened? I love skiing.
       A: Me, too.
    2. **A:** I hurt my arm yesterday.
       B: Oh, no! **Cool! / What happened?**
       A: I fell off my bike.
    3. **A:** I went to a judo competition yesterday.
       B: How was it? / Really? Why?
       A: My brother was in it.
    4. **A:** We went windsurfing yesterday.
       B: Nice! **How was it? / Really?**
       A: It was fantastic!

PROGRESS CHECK: Now I can . . .

☐ identify different sports and activities.
☐ ask and answer *yes/no* questions about past events.
☐ ask and answer *Wh-* questions about past events.
☐ express interest in what someone is saying.
☐ write a short biography.
☐ talk about traditional sports events.

10 Vacation: Here and There

Discovery EDUCATION

BE CURIOUS

- City of Water
- Where do you like going on vacation?
- Alaska!
- Big Art

1. Where do you think the diver is?
2. What does she see?
3. Do you want to do this?

UNIT CONTENTS

Vocabulary Weather, months, and seasons; landforms
Grammar be going to; superlative adjectives
Listening A conversation about a trip to Ecuador

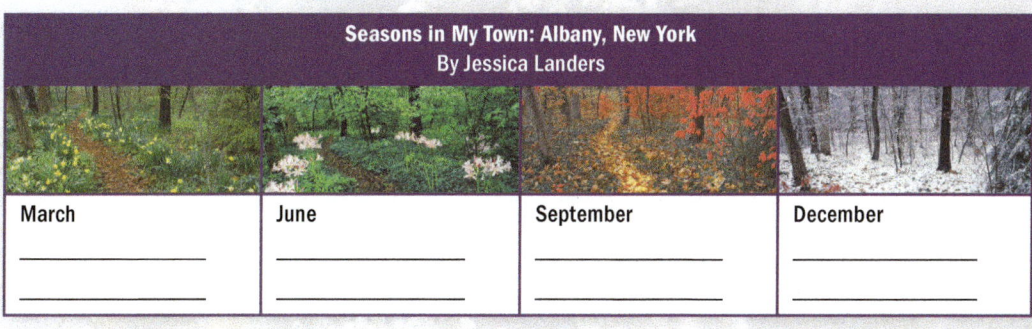

Vocabulary: Weather, months, and seasons

1. **What's the weather like? Write the sentences next to the correct numbers.**

   It's cloudy.   It's icy.   It's snowy.   It's sunny.
   It's foggy.   It's rainy. It's stormy.   It's windy.

   1. _It's icy._
   2. _____
   3. _____
   4. _____
   5. _____
   6. _____
   7. _____
   8. _____

2. **Listen, check, and repeat.**

3. **Complete the chart with the correct months. Then listen to Jessica talk about the seasons where she lives, and check your answers.**

   Seasons in My Town: Albany, New York
   By Jessica Landers

March	June	September	December
_____	_____	_____	_____
_____	_____	_____	_____

   April
   August
   February
   January
   July
   May
   November
   October

4. **YOUR TURN** Work with a partner. What is the weather like in your city or town for each season or month?

   > We don't have four seasons. We have the rainy season and the dry season.

   > You're right. The rainy season usually starts in May. In May, it's warm and very rainy. In June, . . .

Speaking: Your favorite time of year

5. **YOUR TURN** Work with a partner. Discuss your favorite month, season, and kind of weather. Why are they your favorites?

   > What's your favorite month?
   > February.
   > Why do you like February?
   > Well, my birthday is February 14.

6. **Join another pair. Tell them about your partner's favorite month, season, and kind of weather.**

   > Nick's favorite month is February because his birthday is in that month. His favorite season is . . .

   ▶ Workbook, p. 64

Reading Wish You Were Here; My Trip to Brazil; Canada: Land of Surprises
Conversation Making suggestions
Writing An email about a vacation

VACATION PLANS
Wish You Were Here...

a **Penguins in Patagonia**

b **A Home Away From Home**

c **A Magical Ride**

1

Hi Mom and Dad,

Brent and I are having a great time in Florida with Grandma and Grandpa. It's sunny and very hot. Disney World is amazing! Today, we swam with sharks at the Disney water park. Tomorrow, Brent and I are going to go on every ride! Of course, Grandma and Grandpa aren't going to go on the roller coasters. See you next week!

Miss you,
Becca

2

Hey, Jeff!

I'm in Thailand with my family. We're in a tree house in the jungle. It's really cool. Yesterday, we rode elephants and went on a night safari! Next, we're going to stay in a hotel near the beach. I'm going to swim every day, and I'm going to go scuba diving!

Your friend,
Carla

3

Hello Aunt Rita,

The wildlife in Patagonia is great! Patagonia is a beautiful place in Argentina with a lot of interesting animals: penguins, sea lions, whales, and more! I took a lot of pictures today. I'm going to put them online tomorrow.

See you soon,
Ivan

DID YOU KNOW...?
Over 16 million people visit Disney World every year. The parking lot has spaces for 75,000 cars per day.

Reading: Descriptions of vacations

1. Look at the photos. Where do you think these places are? Which place do you want to visit?

2. Read and listen to the postcards. Match the backs of the postcards (1–3) to the fronts of the postcards (a–c).

   1. ____   2. ____   3. ____

3. Read the article again. Whose postcard mentions these things? Write *B* (Becca), *C* (Carla), or *I* (Ivan). Sometimes more than one answer is possible.

   1. staying in more than one place ___C___
   2. the weather _____
   3. swimming _____
   4. seeing animals _____
   5. taking pictures _____

4. **YOUR TURN** Work with a partner. What other things do you think you can do in the places in the postcards? Why?

   > You can go windsurfing in Patagonia. My friend went one time, and she loved it.

96 | Unit 10

Grammar: *be going to*

5. Complete the chart.

Use *be going to* to talk about future plans.	
Wh- questions and answers	**Yes/No questions and answers**
Where **are** you **going to go** on vacation? I**'m going to go** to the beach. I**'m not** _____ to the mountains.	**Are** you _____ to go to the beach? Yes, **I am**. No, **I'm not**.
When **is** Ivan **going to put** photos online? He _____ them online tomorrow. He**'s not going to put** them online tonight.	_____ he **going to put** photos online? Yes, he **is**. No, he _____.
What _____ they **going to do** tomorrow? Brent and Carla **are going to ride** every ride. Their grandparents _____ **ride** roller coasters.	**Are** they **going to ride** roller coasters? Yes, they _____. No, they **aren't**.
Common time expressions: tomorrow, tonight, this weekend, next week/month/year	

▶ Check your answers: Grammar reference, p. 115

6. Write questions and answers with *be going to*.

1. Tom / go / to Spain (no, Egypt)

   Q: *Is Tom going to go to Spain?*

   A: *No, he's not. He's going to go to Egypt.*

2. you / study / French (no, Japanese)

   Q: _____

   A: _____

3. Donna and Jess / ride / elephants in India (yes)

   Q: _____

   A: _____

4. who / you / study / with this weekend (my teammates)

   Q: _____

   A: _____

5. where / you / go / tomorrow (the beach)

   Q: _____

   A: _____

6. what / your friends / do / tonight (go to the movies)

   Q: _____

   A: _____

Say it RIGHT!
🔊 10.04

In informal English, we sometimes reduce *going to* to /gənə/. Listen and repeat the formal and informal versions of the questions in Exercise 6.

Speaking: What's your next adventure?

7. YOUR TURN Work with a partner. Plan a vacation together. Where are you going to go? What are you going to do? Tell the class about your vacation.

> We're going to go to Mexico. We're going to see pyramids. We're also going to swim in the ocean. We're . . .

BE CURIOUS 🔑 Find out about a popular city in Italy. How do people get around there? (Workbook, p. 90)

Discovery EDUCATION

10.1 CITY OF WATER

▶ Workbook, pp. 64–65

The Best VACATION!

Listening: I liked it all!

1. Where was your last vacation? What was the weather like?

2. Listen to Veronica telling Liam about her trip to Ecuador. Match the places with the weather.

   1. Quito _____
   2. Chimborazo _____
   3. Lago Agrio _____
   4. Otavalo _____

   a. cool (not hot and not cold)
   b. really hot
   c. warm and sunny
   d. icy and snowy

3. Listen again. Are the sentences true (T) or false (F)?

   1. Ecuador has a rainy season and a dry season. _____
   2. Veronica climbed a mountain. _____
   3. Veronica saw gray dolphins. _____
   4. Veronica went swimming in Salinas. _____
   5. Veronica's flight was on time. _____

Vocabulary: Landforms

4. Match the words with the pictures. Then listen and check your answers.

   1. _g_ a beach
   2. _____ a desert
   3. _____ a forest
   4. _____ a lake
   5. _____ a hill
   6. _____ a jungle
   7. _____ a river
   8. _____ an ocean
   9. _____ mountains

5. Work with a partner. Where can you find the landforms in Exercise 4 in your country? Which landforms *can't* you find in your country?

   There are a lot of beaches in our country.

   Yes, there are. There are beaches in Cancun and . . .

Grammar: Superlative adjectives

6. Complete the chart.

Use superlative adjectives to compare three or more things.		
1 syllable	long → **the** long**est**	It's **the** _____ river in South America
2 or more syllables	popular → **the most** popular	It's _____ beach in Ecuador.
Ending in consonant + -y	dry → _____	The Atacama Desert is **the driest** place in the world.
	rainy → **the** rain**iest**	Spring is _____ season.
Irregular	good → **the best** bad → **the worst**	What was **the best** place? The airport was _____.

> Check your answers: Grammar reference, p. 115

7. Complete the paragraphs with the superlative forms of the adjectives.

What's ¹ _the best_ (good) place for a beach vacation? Hawaii! Hawaii has some of ² _____ (beautiful) beaches in the world. There are eight main islands. Hawaii Island is ³ _____ (big). Lanai is ⁴ _____ (quiet) island. There aren't any traffic lights! Many people think Maui has ⁵ _____ (pretty) beaches.

December is ⁶ _____ (popular) time to go to Hawaii, and it's also ⁷ _____ (expensive). The weather is ⁸ _____ (good) in the spring and the fall, and it's also ⁹ _____ (cheap) time to go. When's ¹⁰ _____ (bad) time to visit Hawaii? There isn't really a bad time. It's always beautiful in Hawaii!

8. Look at the chart. Write sentences about the mountains with the superlative forms of the adjectives.

	Height	Average temperature	Number of days it rains per year
Chimborazo	4,123 meters	14°C	88
Kilimanjaro	5,892 meters	10°C	72
Mount Everest	8,850 meters	−15°C	58
Mount McKinley	6,194 meters	−6°C	100

1. (high) _Mount Everest is the highest mountain._
2. (cold) _____
3. (warm) _____
4. (wet) _____
5. (dry) _____

Speaking: The best places

9. YOUR TURN Work with a partner. A friend is coming to your country for vacation. What are the best landforms to see and why? Discuss your ideas. Choose the top five places.

> I think Bondi Beach is the best beach.

> I agree. And Blue Lake is the best lake because . . .

10. Join another pair. Share your top five landforms. Did you choose the same places? Decide on the top three places.

> Bondi Beach is the best beach. You can swim in the ocean. Blue Lake is the prettiest lake. It's on an island. The Great Sandy Desert is the most . . .

> Workbook, pp. 66–67

REAL TALK 10.2 WHERE DO YOU LIKE GOING ON VACATION?

Vacation SPOTS

Conversation: Making suggestions

1. **REAL TALK** Watch or listen to the teenagers. Check (✓) the places and activities they talk about.

   Places
   - ☐ the jungle
   - ☐ beaches
   - ☐ an island
   - ☐ a river
   - ☐ a lake

   Activities
   - ☐ scuba diving
   - ☐ swimming
   - ☐ inline skating
   - ☐ snorkeling
   - ☐ snowboarding
   - ☐ skateboarding
   - ☐ skiing
   - ☐ windsurfing
   - ☐ biking

2. **YOUR TURN** Where do *you* like to go on vacation? Tell your partner.

3. Listen to Mia and Dan picking a vacation spot. Complete the conversation.

   USEFUL LANGUAGE: Making suggestions
   Let's | We can | What about | Why don't we

   Mia: Can you believe it? Mom and Dad are letting us pick our vacation spot this year!
   Dan: I know. Where do we want to go?
   Mia: ¹_____ go somewhere warm.
   Dan: OK. ²_____ going to **the beach**?
   Mia: No. That's boring! We went to **the beach** last year.
   Dan: ³_____ go to **the desert**?
   Mia: Hmm.... That's a good idea.
   Dan: Yeah. ⁴_____ **go hiking**.
   Mia: Oh, and **sandboarding**!
   Dan: That sounds exciting!
   Mia: Great! We're going to the **desert**! I'm going to tell Mom and Dad.

   > **Get it RIGHT!**
   > Don't forget the apostrophe in *let's*.
   > **Let's** *go somewhere cool.*
   > NOT: ~~Lets go somewhere cool.~~
   > **Let's = let us,** but people almost always use the contraction, not the full form.

   > **NOTICE IT**
   > Use the base form of a verb after *Why don't we* and the *-ing* form after *What about*.
   > *Why don't we* **go** *to the Amazon rainforest?*
   > *What about* **going** *to the Amazon rainforest?*

4. Practice the conversation with a partner.

5. **YOUR TURN** Repeat the conversation in Exercise 3, but change the words in **purple**. Use your own ideas.

To: paulap@net.cup/org
From: simon99@net.cup/org
Subject: My Trip to Brazil

Hi Paula,

Thanks for your email. The photos of your dog are great! I'm going to show them to my mom. She loves dogs! Guess what? I'm going to visit Brazil for the whole month of July! July is one of the coldest months in Brazil, but it's still warm. My parents, my sister, my grandpa, and I are going to fly to Rio first. We're going to stay with my dad's friend, Cristiano, there. Then we're going to drive south to a city called Paraty. Both cities have beaches and mountains, so we're going to swim in the ocean and go hiking a lot. I can't wait! Do you have any vacation plans?

Your friend,
Simon

Reading to write: Simon's email about a vacation

6. Look at the photo. Which things will Simon see in Brazil? Read the email to check.

beaches	mountains	cities	the ocean
hills	the desert	a river	

Focus on CONTENT
In an email about a future vacation, include this information about where you're going to go and what you're going to do:
- activities
- lodging (hotel, house)
- place(s)
- people with you
- the time of year
- transportation
- the weather

7. Read the email again. What information did Simon include for each category in the Focus on Content box?

Focus on LANGUAGE
Starting and ending an email
An email to a friend can start with a sentence that:
- mentions a previous email: *I got your email, thanks.*
- asks how someone is: *How are you?*

It can end with a sentence that:
- asks someone to respond: *Please write back.*
- asks someone a question: *What are you going to do this weekend?*
- wishes someone well: *I hope all is well.*

8. How does Simon start and finish his email? Which categories from the Focus on Language box does he use?

9. Read the sentences to start or finish an email. Which category from the Focus on Language box do they belong to?

1. Email me soon! _____
2. Thanks for writing. _____
3. When are you going to visit me? _____
4. I hope you're enjoying your summer. _____

Writing: An email about a vacation

PLAN
Make notes in the questionnaire about a future vacation.

> Where are you going to go?
> When are you going to go?
> What's the weather going to be like?
> Who are you going to go with?
> How are you going to get there?
> Where are you going to stay?
> What are you going to see and do?

WRITE
Now write an email to a friend about your vacation. Use your notes to help you. Write at least 80 words.

CHECK
Check your writing. Can you answer "yes" to these questions?

- Is information from the Focus on Content box in your email?
- Do you start and end your email with appropriate sentences?

CANADA:
A Land of Surprises

Canada is an enormous country, but only 35 million people live there. Here are some interesting facts about Canada, a land of many different and beautiful landscapes.

a The Nunavut Province is close to the Arctic Circle. It's always cold, snowy, and icy there. Temperatures get down to −37°C in the winter! The license plates on their cars are in the shape of polar bears. Can you guess why?

b The symbol of Canada is the maple leaf. It's on the country's flag. These leaves are red in the fall.

c There are a lot of beautiful parks, lakes, and mountains in Canada. The biggest lake in the world is Lake Superior on Canada's border with the US.

d The Rocky Mountains in the west are amazing, but if you're going to go there, be careful of the bears!

e The CN Tower in Toronto is the tallest tower in Canada. It's 553 meters high, and it has a restaurant on the top!

f Niagara Falls is one of the most famous waterfalls in the world. Almost 30 million people visit it every year. It is really three waterfalls: the American, Bridal Veil, and Horseshoe falls.

g About 20 percent of the population is bilingual in English and French (the official languages).

Culture: Interesting facts about Canada

1. Look at the photos. What do you see?

2. Read and listen to the article. Match the topics (1–7) with the paragraphs (a–g).

   1. A national symbol ____
   2. Canada's languages ____
   3. A famous waterfall ____
   4. An enormous lake ____
   5. Toronto's tower ____
   6. Snow all year ____
   7. Beware of the bears. ____

3. Read the article again. Write the correct place or thing for each statement.

   1. Lots of people visit it every year. _____
   2. It is on the Canadian flag. _____
   3. They are on cars in Nunavut. _____
   4. These are two languages that 20 percent of the population speaks. _____
   5. There are black bears here. _____

4. **YOUR TURN** Work with a partner. What are some interesting facts about your country?

   > K2 is the name of a famous mountain here. It's the second highest mountain in the world.

DID YOU KNOW...?
About 95 percent of the people in Quebec, Canada, speak French.

BE CURIOUS Find out about Alaska. What is a glacier? (Workbook, p. 91)

10.3 ALASKA!

UNIT 10 REVIEW

Vocabulary

1. Match the pictures with the weather.

   a b c
   d e f
   g h

   1. _h_ foggy
   2. ____ cloudy
   3. ____ icy
   4. ____ rainy
   5. ____ snowy
   6. ____ stormy
   7. ____ sunny
   8. ____ windy

2. Complete the sentences with the correct words.

   | beach | desert | forest | hill | ocean | river |

   1. My brother loves surfing in the _____. He likes to ride really big waves!
   2. It's hot and very dry in the _____.
   3. Let's play on the _____ before we go swimming.
   4. It's easy to walk up this _____. It's not very high.
   5. There are a lot of tall trees in the _____.
   6. We took a boat ride down a _____ yesterday.

Grammar

3. Complete the conversation with the correct forms of *be going to*.

   Owen: What ¹_____ (you / do) this summer?
   Alex: ²_____ (I / go) to Alaska.
   Owen: That's cool! Who ³_____ (you / travel) with?
   Alex: My aunt, uncle, and cousins. ⁴_____ (we / fly) to Anchorage in June.
   Owen: Where ⁵_____ (you / stay)?
   Alex: My aunt has friends in Anchorage, so ⁶_____ (we / sleep) at their house. ⁷_____ (her friends / take) us all over Alaska!

4. Complete the sentences with the superlative forms of the adjectives.

   1. Tokyo is _____ (big) city in Japan.
   2. The Nile is _____ (long) river in the world.
   3. I think the beach is _____ (relaxing) place for a vacation.
   4. That restaurant has _____ (good) Mexican food.
   5. Spring is _____ (storm) season here.
   6. I think winter is _____ (bad) time to travel.

Useful language

5. Correct the mistakes.

   1. **A:** What should we do in Seoul?
      B: Why don't we going to a night market?
   2. **A:** I can't wait to go to the jungle!
      B: I know. We can't go hiking and see a lot of animals.
      A: That sounds fun!
   3. **A:** What do you want to do tomorrow?
      B: What about swim in the ocean?
   4. **A:** Where should we go for our spring vacation?
      B: Lets go to a beach in Maine.

PROGRESS CHECK: Now I can . . .

- ☐ talk about weather, seasons, and months.
- ☐ discuss vacation plans.
- ☐ describe different landforms and places to visit.
- ☐ make suggestions.
- ☐ write an email about future plans.
- ☐ share interesting facts about my country.

UNITS 9–10 REVIEW, Workbook, pp. 70–71

CLIL PROJECT
10.4 Big Art, p. 120

Uncover Your Knowledge
UNITS 6–10 Review Game

TEAM 1 START

- What's happening in your class right now? Make five sentences in 30 seconds.
- What season are you in? What is the weather today? Is it typical?
- Find out what your teammate did last weekend. Ask two Wh- questions and two yes/no questions.
- How do you get to school? What transportation do you take?
- What are three things you *didn't* do when you were a child? Tell a partner in 30 seconds.
- Describe a typical dinner at your house. What food is in it? How often do you have it?
- Tell your partner two pieces of exciting news. Use different expressions for each piece of news.
- Name 10 different sports or activities in 30 seconds.
- Make five sentences about places in your city or town. Use superlative adjectives.
- Give examples of three pets and three wild animals in 15 seconds.
- How can you express interest in a conversation? Give three examples.

INSTRUCTIONS:
- Make teams and choose game pieces.
- Put your game pieces on your team's START.
- Flip a coin to see who goes first.
- Read the first challenge. Can you do it correctly?

   Yes ➔ Continue to the next challenge.

   No ➔ Lose your turn.

The first team to do all of the challenges wins!

- GRAMMAR
- VOCABULARY
- USEFUL LANGUAGE

TEAM 2
START

- Make four sentences about the last party you went to. Use *there was/were*.
- Role-play a conversation with your teammate. Order a meal and a drink in a restaurant.
- In one minute, say four things you are going to do this evening.
- Describe your favorite animal. Where does it live? Why do you like it?
- What's in your refrigerator at home? Make five sentences with *there is/are* and *some/any* in one minute.
- Give examples of six different landforms.
- Say three fun things and one boring thing you did last weekend.
- Role-play a conversation with your teammate. Ask for and give directions to the bathroom.
- Name five things that you can wear at the gym.
- In 30 seconds, make three sentences about sports. Use *play*, *do*, and *go*.
- Imagine that you are at the zoo. Describe what the animals are doing. Give four examples.
- Plan a vacation with your teammate. Make suggestions for three different things to do.
- In one minute, name six different places you can usually find in a town or city.
- In 30 seconds, give examples of five foods from plants and five foods from animals.

Units 6–10 Review | 105

a/an; some and any with countable and uncountable nouns, p. 57

Use a/an or numbers to express quantity with countable nouns. Don't use a/an or numbers with uncountable nouns. Use some and any with both countable and uncountable nouns.

Countable nouns		Uncountable nouns
a panda	**two** panda**s**	chicken, cheese, corn
an animal	**three** animal**s**	
Do you have **any vegetables**? Yes, I have **some vegetables**. No, I don't have any **vegetables**.		Does she have **any rice**? Yes, she has **some rice**. No, she doesn't have **any rice**.

1. Complete the conversations with *a, an, some,* or *any*.

1. **A:** Do you want _____ cake?

   B: Yes, I'd like _____ cake, please.

2. **A:** Do we have _____ eggs in the fridge?

   B: Yes, we have _____ eggs.

3. **A:** Do you have _____ carrots in your lunch?

   B: No, I don't have _____ carrots, but I have _____ oranges and _____ apple.

there is/are with much, many, and a lot of, p. 59

Use there is/are with much, many, and a lot of to express quantity.

Countable nouns	How **many** crackers **are there**? **There are** four crackers. **There are a lot of** crackers. = **There are many** crackers. **There aren't a lot of** crackers. = **There aren't many** crackers. **Are there any** crackers? Yes, **there are**. = **There are some** crackers. No, **there aren't**. = **There aren't any** crackers.
Uncountable nouns	How **much** bread **is there**? **There are** two slices of bread. **There's a lot of** bread. **There isn't a lot of** bread. = **There isn't much** bread. **Is there any** bread? Yes, **there is**. = There is some bread. No, **there isn't**. = There isn't any bread.
Contraction:	There is = **There's**

2. Circle the correct answers.

1. How **many / much / a lot of** tacos do you want?

2. There **is / isn't / are / aren't** any soup left.

3. There aren't **many / much / any** burgers. I think there are only two left.

4. There **is / isn't / are / aren't** three oranges on the table. You can have one.

5. There isn't **many / much / any** ice cream here. There's only enough for one person.

6. **Is / Isn't / Are / Aren't** there any cheese on your salad?

Present continuous, p. 67

Use the present continuous to talk about activities that are happening now.

Wh- questions (do)	Affirmative (play)	Negative (dance)
What **am** I **doing**?	You**'re playing**.	You **aren't dancing**.
What **are** you **doing**?	I**'m playing**.	I**'m not dancing**.
What **is** he/she/it **doing**?	He/she/it **is playing**.	He/she/it **isn't dancing**.
What **are** we/they **doing**?	We/they **are playing**.	We/they **aren't dancing**.

Yes/No questions (eat)	Short answers	
Am I **eating**?	Yes, you **are**.	No, you **aren't**.
Are you **eating**?	Yes, I **am**.	No, I**'m not**.
Is he/she/it **eating**?	Yes, he/she/it **is**.	No, he/she/it **isn't**.
Are they/we **eating**?	Yes, they/we **are**.	No, they/we **aren't**.

1. Write sentences in the present continuous.

1. the cow / eat / grass / . _____
2. the hippo / not / sleep / . _____
3. I / feed / the horses / . _____
4. the cats / sit / in the sun / ? _____
5. we / play / with the dogs / . _____
6. where / the giraffe / go / ? _____

Simple present vs. present continuous, page 69

Use the simple present for facts, habits, and routines.	Use the present continuous to talk about activities that are happening now.
Simple present	**Present continuous**
What **do** monkeys **eat**? They usually **eat** bananas.	What **is** that monkey **eating**? It **is eating** a banana at the moment.
Do you **go** to the zoo? Yes, I **do**. I **go** to the zoo once a year.	**Are** you **going** to the zoo? Yes, I **am**. I**'m going** to the zoo right now.
Common time expressions	
always, usually, often, sometimes, never once a week, twice a month, every year on Mondays, on weekends	now right now at the moment

2. Complete the sentences with the simple present or present continuous forms of the verbs.

1. Where _____ tigers usually _____ (hunt)?
2. Yoli _____ (feed) the pigs right now.
3. Marcus _____ (walk) his dog every day.
4. _____ you _____ (watch) the TV show about polar bears right now?
5. Sharks _____ (not have) legs or arms.
6. Those dogs _____ (work) at the moment.

> **Get it RIGHT!**
>
> Here are some more verbs that we usually use in the simple present, not the present continuous.
> **Possession**: have, own
> **Senses**: see, feel, hear, taste, smell
> **Feelings**: love, like, hate
> **Thoughts**: understand, know, think
> **Other**: be, want
> John **has** two cats.
> NOT ~~John's having two cats~~.

112 | Unit 7

Simple past of *be* and *there was/were*, p. 77

Use the simple past of be and there was/were to describe things in the past.

	Singular	Plural
Simple past of *be*	What **was** Pompeii like? It **was** very busy. It **wasn't** small. Was Pompeii busy? Yes, it **was**. / No, it **wasn't**	What **were** the people like? They **were** rich. They **weren't** poor. **Were** the people rich? Yes, they **were**. / No, they **weren't**.
	I — **was** you — **were** he/she/it — **was**	we — **were** you — **were** they — **were**
There was/were	What huge building **was there**? **There was** an amphitheater. **There wasn't** a fitness center. **Was there** an amphitheater? Yes, **there was**. / No, **there wasn't**.	What kind of buildings **were there**? **There were** stores and schools. **There weren't** any airports. **Were there** any stores? Yes, **there were**. / No, **there weren't**.

1. Circle the correct answers.

1. Where **was / were** you yesterday?
2. I **wasn't / weren't** at the skate park yesterday.
3. **There was / There were** a museum on that street.
4. **Was there / Were there** any clothes at the market?
5. Tom, Jack, and Hilda **wasn't / weren't** in class today.
6. **There wasn't / There weren't** any cars in the parking lot.

Simple past statements with regular and irregular verbs, p. 79

Use simple past statements to talk about past events and activities.

	Subject	Affirmative	Negative
Regular	I/you/he/she/it/we/they	**stayed** with a family. **studied** Spanish. **liked** the hat. **shopped** at the market.	**didn't stay** in a hotel. **didn't study** Quechua. **didn't like** the game. **didn't shop** at the mall.
Irregular	I/you/he/she/it/we/they	**bought** a hat. **went** to Peru. **took** buses and taxis.	**didn't buy** a blanket. **didn't go** to Chile. **didn't take** the subway.

2. Complete the sentences with the simple past forms of the correct verbs.

> arrive   go   play   see   shop   study

1. We _____ soccer at the fitness center for three hours yesterday.
2. Jenny _____ a great movie on TV last night.
3. The bus was late. It _____ on time.
4. I _____ to Chicago a month ago.
5. My dad and I _____ at a market yesterday. It was fun!
6. I can't speak Portuguese because I _____ it in school.

Simple past yes/no questions and short answers, p. 87

Use simple past yes/no questions to find out if events or activities happened in the past or not.

Yes/No questions		
Did	I/you/he/she/it/we/they	**go** to the game last night?
Short answers		
Yes,	I/you/he/she/it/we/they	**did.**
No,		**didn't.**

1. **Write questions in the simple past. Then match the questions with the answers.**

    1. wrestlers / compete / on Saturday
       Did the wrestlers compete on Saturday?
    2. you / play / soccer yesterday
       _____
    3. Victoria / buy / a skateboard
       _____
    4. I / make / the basketball team
       _____
    5. Greg / wear / his new hoodie / last night
       _____

    a. No, we didn't.
    b. Yes, you did.
    c. No, he didn't.
    d. Yes, they did.
    e. Yes, she did.

Simple past Wh- questions, p. 89

Use simple past Wh- questions to ask for information about past events and activities.

Question word (+ noun)	did	Subject	Base verb (+ phrase)
What		you	**do**?
Who		Vicky	**watch**?
How	did	Barry	**get** to the game?
When		it	**rain**?
Where		they	**go**?
How many points		our team	**score**?

2. **Put the words in order to make Wh- questions in the simple past. Use the correct forms of the verbs.**

    1. Carol / when / play / volleyball *When did Carol play volleyball?*
    2. buy / new shorts / you / why _____
    3. to the game / get / how / they _____
    4. that sweatshirt / Jim / where / buy _____
    5. see / you / who / at the game _____
    6. the team / take / which bus _____

be going to, p. 97

Use be going to to talk about future plans.

Wh- questions and answers	Yes/No questions and answers
Where **are** you **going to go** on vacation? I**'m going to go** to the beach. I**'m not going to go** to the mountains.	**Are** you **going to go** to the beach? Yes, I **am**. No, I**'m not**.
When **is** he/she/it **going to put** photos online? He/She/It **is going to put** them online tomorrow. He**'s**/She**'s**/It**'s not going to put** them online tonight.	**Is** he/she/it **going to put** photos online? Yes, he/she/it **is**. No, he/she/it **isn't**.
What **are** they/we/you **going to do** tomorrow? They/we/you **are going to ride** every ride. They/we/you **aren't going to ride** roller coasters.	**Are** they/we/you **going to ride** roller coasters? Yes, they/we/you **are**. No, they/we/you **aren't**.

Common time expressions: tomorrow, tonight, this weekend, next week/month/year

1. Put the words in the correct order to make sentences with *be going to*. Use the correct forms of the verbs.

1. in Brazil / where / stay / you / ?
   Where are you going to stay in Brazil?

2. to the beach / go / tomorrow / she / .
   _____

3. the mountains / not hike / we / in / .
   _____

4. in / Marcos / the ocean / swim / ?
   _____

5. our vacation / not rain / it /on / .
   _____

Superlative adjectives, p. 99

Use superlative adjectives to compare three or more things.

1 syllable	long → **the** long**est** nice → **the** nic**est** big → **the** big**gest**	It's **the longest river** in South America. This is **the nicest** hotel in the city. Tokyo is **the biggest** city in Japan.
2 or more syllables	popular → **the most** popular relaxing → **the most** relaxing *Note:* Some 2-syllable words have two correct superlative forms. quiet → **the most** quiet / quiet**est**	It's **the most popular** beach in Ecuador. Where is **the most relaxing** beach?
Ending in consonant + -y	dry → **the** dri**est** rainy → **the** rain**iest**	The Atacama Desert is **the driest** place in the world. Spring is **the rainiest** season.
Irregular	good → **the best** bad → **the worst**	What was **the best** place? The airport was **the worst**.

2. Complete the sentences with the superlative forms of the adjectives.

1. When is _____ (good) time to go to Australia?
2. February is _____ (cloudy) month in my town.
3. Summer is _____ (hot) season here.
4. Winter is _____ (bad) time to travel.
5. Where's _____ (safe) place to stay in this city?

This page intentionally left blank.

Where does it GROW?

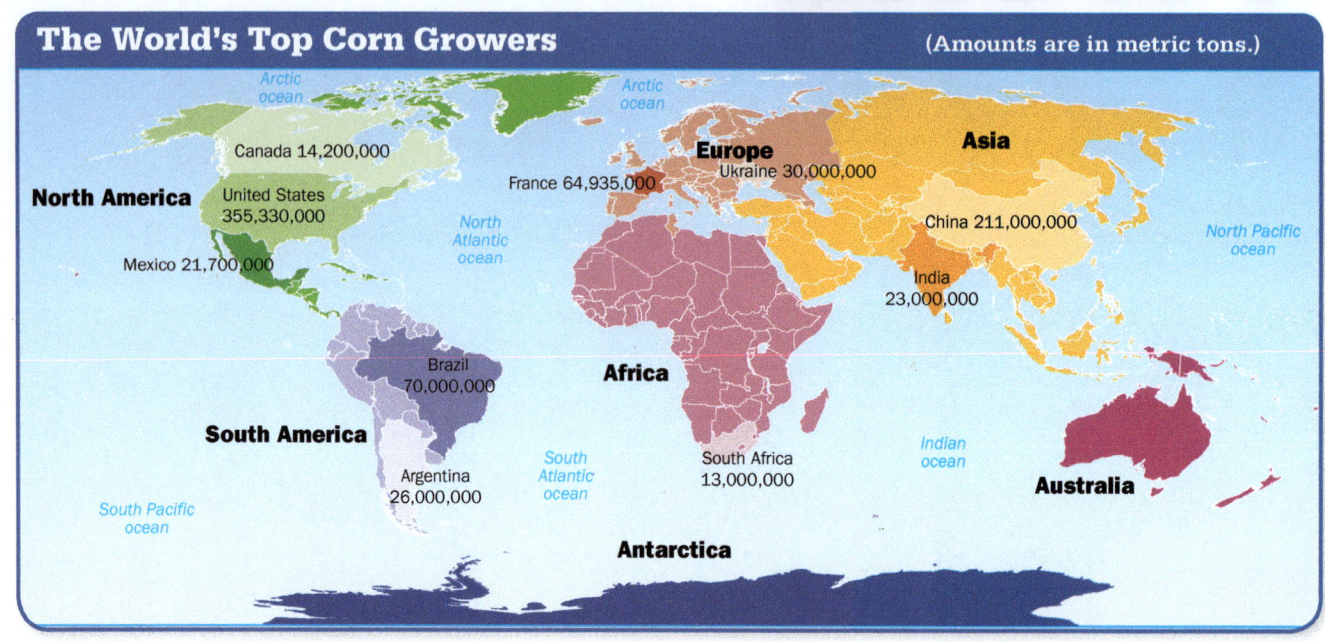

The World's Top Corn Growers (Amounts are in metric tons.)

- Canada 14,200,000
- United States 355,330,000
- Mexico 21,700,000
- France 64,935,000
- Ukraine 30,000,000
- China 211,000,000
- India 23,000,000
- Brazil 70,000,000
- Argentina 26,000,000
- South Africa 13,000,000

1. Look at the map. Answer the questions.

1. Which country grows the most corn?
2. What is the only country in Africa that is a top grower?
3. Which continent grows the most corn?

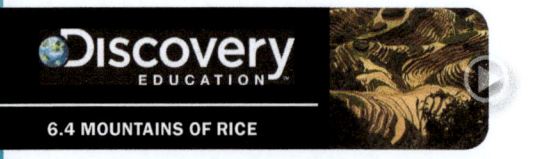

Discovery EDUCATION
6.4 MOUNTAINS OF RICE

2. Watch the video. Circle the correct answers.

1. Where is Long Shen?
   a. China   b. Vietnam   c. Japan
2. From April to October, it is _____ in Long Shen.
   a. hot and dry   b. cold and rainy   c. hot and rainy
3. Rice plants need a lot of _____.
   a. milk   b. water   c. juice
4. Chinese people do not eat much _____.
   a. soup   b. corn   c. bread
5. What do families in Long Shen usually do in the evening?
   a. watch TV   b. eat dinner   c. play games

PROJECT Choose a fruit, vegetable, or grain. Label or color a map to show where it grows. Present your map to the class. Answer the questions.

- Where does the food grow? Name the continents and the countries.
- Why does the food grow there? Give examples of things that affect the food's growth.
- Do the people from those places eat a lot of the food? Who else eats a lot of it?

Chameleons and Other REPTILES

Not Your Average Pet

Now, not everybody loves reptiles, but they are an important part of the animal kingdom. What makes them so special, you ask? Read on.

Reptiles are born on land from _____. Their body temperature changes to match their environment, so they are called _____ animals. Can you imagine that? When it's cold outside, they're cold, too!

Reptiles are _____—they have backbones. Also, like fish, they have _____ on their skin. Most of them, have four _____. Also, reptiles have a _____, which is sometimes a different color than the rest of their body. This is to confuse their enemies.

There are many different and unusual animals on Earth, and reptiles—scary or not—are a special part of it!

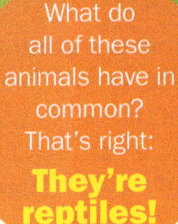

What do all of these animals have in common? That's right: **They're reptiles!**

1. Look at the pictures in the article. What animals are these?

2. Complete the article with the correct words.   cold-blooded   eggs   legs   scales   tail   vertebrates

3. Label the picture of the Komodo dragon with the correct words.

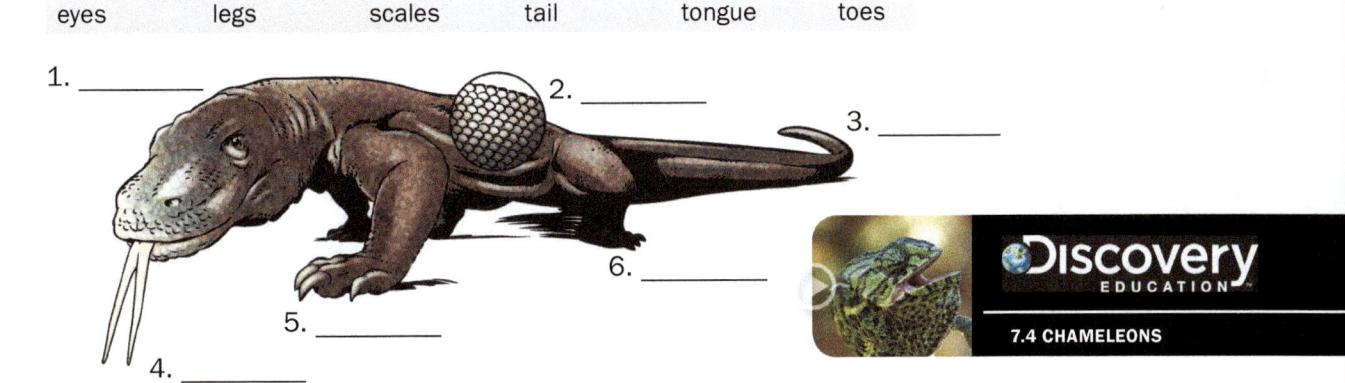

   eyes   legs   scales   tail   tongue   toes

   1. _____
   2. _____
   3. _____
   4. _____
   5. _____
   6. _____

Discovery EDUCATION
7.4 CHAMELEONS

4. Watch the video. Are the sentences true (*T*) or false (*F*)?

   1. The Mediterranean Chameleon can point its eyes in two directions. ____
   2. Chameleons climb trees with their special toes. ____
   3. Chameleons don't have scales. ____
   4. Chameleons are able to change color. ____
   5. All chameleons are large. ____
   6. Chameleons have short tails. ____
   7. Chameleons catch food with their tongues. ____
   8. All chameleons are reptiles. ____

PROJECT   Choose a reptile. Answer the questions. Present your information to the class. Use pictures in your presentation.

- Where does the reptile live?
- What does it eat?
- Does the reptile have any special skills or traits? Describe them.

Unit 7 | CLIL Project | 119

CLIL PROJECT

Say it with ART!

Top: This is a **statue** of a king. It is an ancient **ruin** from Egypt. It is more than 3,000 years old. It's also **huge**: 21 meters tall! Statues are examples of **sculptures**. Sculptures are not flat, like paintings. People make sculptures with different materials, such as wood, clay, metal, or stone.

Bottom: Artists use colors to **express** ideas or feelings. This painting uses a **bright** color: red. Red often means "angry." The painting also has different **shapes**, such as circles, triangles, and rectangles. The shapes are **symbols**. They represent other objects or ideas.

1. **Look at the art and read the descriptions. Match the words in bold with the definitions.**

    1. ___ express
    2. ___ symbol
    3. ___ statue
    4. ___ ruin
    5. ___ huge
    6. ___ sculpture
    7. ___ shape
    8. ___ bright

    a. full of light; shiny
    b. show a feeling
    c. very big
    d. a piece of art that is not flat
    e. the form of an object
    f. a sculpture that looks like a person
    g. parts left from an old building or city
    h. something that we use to mean something else

Discovery EDUCATION
10.4 BIG ART

2. **Watch the video. Circle the correct answers.**

    1. What is unusual about the Aztec sculpture?
       a. her tongue   b. her nose   c. her eyes

    2. What does the grandmother first notice about Sebastián's sculptures?
       a. their size   b. their shape   c. their color

    3. Sebastián puts his sculptures in _____.
       a. museums   b. schools   c. public places

    4. Sebastián uses _____ in his studio.
       a. blocks   b. models   c. crystals

PROJECT Create your own art, or create a model of art you want to build. Present it to the class. Answer the questions.

- What shapes and colors does your art have?
- What feelings or ideas does it express? What symbols does it use?
- Where would you like to build it? Why?

Uncover 1 Combo B

Susan Evento

Workbook

CAMBRIDGE UNIVERSITY PRESS

DISCOVERY EDUCATION

6 Time to Eat

VOCABULARY Food

1 Put the letters in the correct order to make food words. Then write the name of each food under its picture.

1. ANANASB _bananas_
2. EANBS _____
3. EESEHC _____
4. DEBAR _____
5. ESOMATOT _____
6. FEBE _____
7. NEKCICH _____
8. RORTACS _____
9. TAPTESOO _____

a _carrots_
b _____ 
c _____ 
d _____ 
e _____ 
f _____ 
g _____ 
h _____ 
i _____ 

2 Circle the correct answers.

1. Which one is a vegetable?
   a. chicken   b. carrots   c. eggs
2. Which one is a fruit?
   a. beans   b. oranges   c. milk
3. Which one do people often eat for breakfast?
   a. beef   b. carrots   c. eggs
4. Which is a food that vegetarians do NOT eat?
   a. fruits   b. beef   c. vegetables

3 Complete the sentences.

| animals | apples | juice | plants |

1. Oranges, bananas, and _____ are fruits.
2. Cheese, eggs, and beef come from _____.
3. Oranges, potatoes, and tomatoes come from _____.
4. Milk, water, and _____ are things to drink.

4 Answer the questions with complete sentences.

1. What are five foods you like to eat?
   I like to eat beef, cheese, potatoes, tomatoes, and oranges.
2. What is your favorite food?
   _____
3. How often do you eat your favorite food?
   _____
4. What are three things you like to drink?
   _____
   _____
5. What is your favorite drink?
   _____
6. How often do you drink your favorite drink?
   _____

GRAMMAR a / an; some and any with countable and uncountable nouns

1 Write each word in the correct column.

apple	burger	corn	meat
banana	~~carrot~~	egg	tomato
bread	cheese	juice	rice

Countable nouns	Uncountable nouns
carrot	

2 Complete the text with *a/an*, *some*, or *any*.

Jeremy plays football. He loves meat, but he doesn't eat a lot of it, and he doesn't eat ¹___any___ takeout food.

Here's what he usually eats:

Breakfast: ²_____ fruit, ³_____ big plate of eggs, ⁴_____ bread, and ⁵_____ milk.

Snack after training: ⁶_____ sports drink and ⁷_____ bananas. He doesn't eat ⁸_____ potato chips.

Lunch: ⁹_____ pizza, ¹⁰_____ apple, and ¹¹_____ water.

Dinner: ¹²_____ fish, a lot of potatoes and ¹³_____ vegetables.

3 Write sentences using *a/an*, *some*, or *any* for three countable and three uncountable nouns in Exercise 1.

1. ___I eat some carrots for lunch every day.___ OR
   ___I eat a carrot for lunch every day.___ OR
   ___I don't eat any carrots.___
2. _____
3. _____
4. _____
5. _____
6. _____
7. _____

Unit 6 | 37

VOCABULARY More food and meals

1 Circle 12 more food words.

sandwichtacossaladsushipastacakeicecreamburgercerealyogurtcrackersnutssoup

2 Write the names of the meals on the timeline.

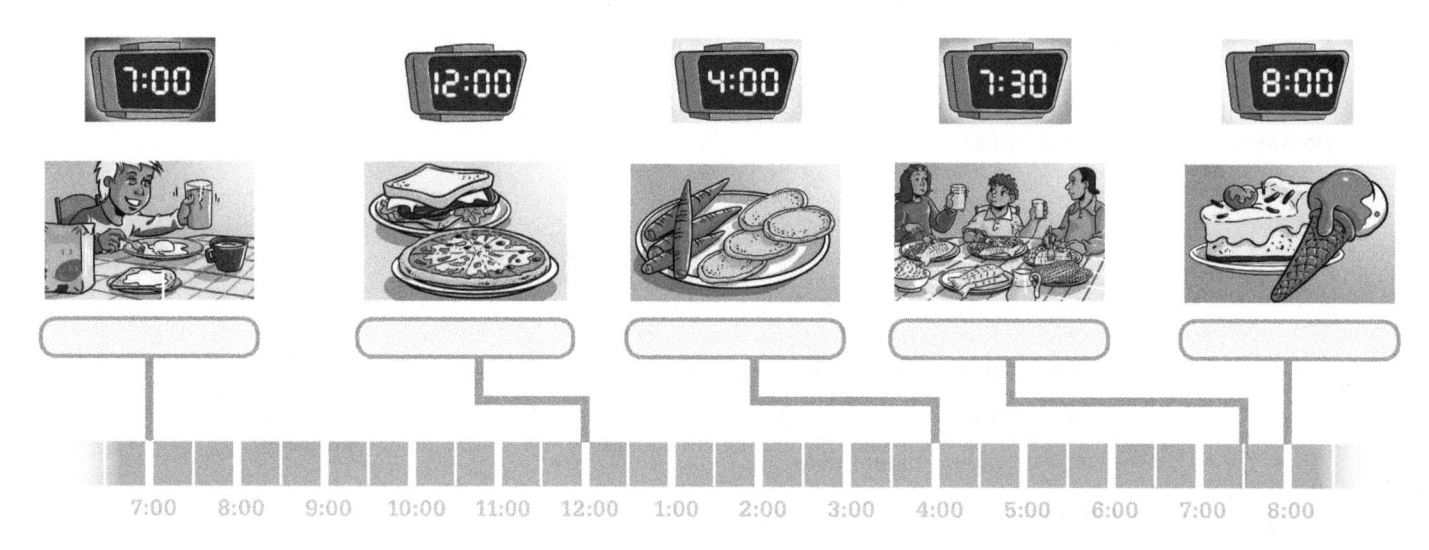

3 What do you eat at meals? Write the food words in the word web. Add your own ideas. Some words can go in more than one circle.

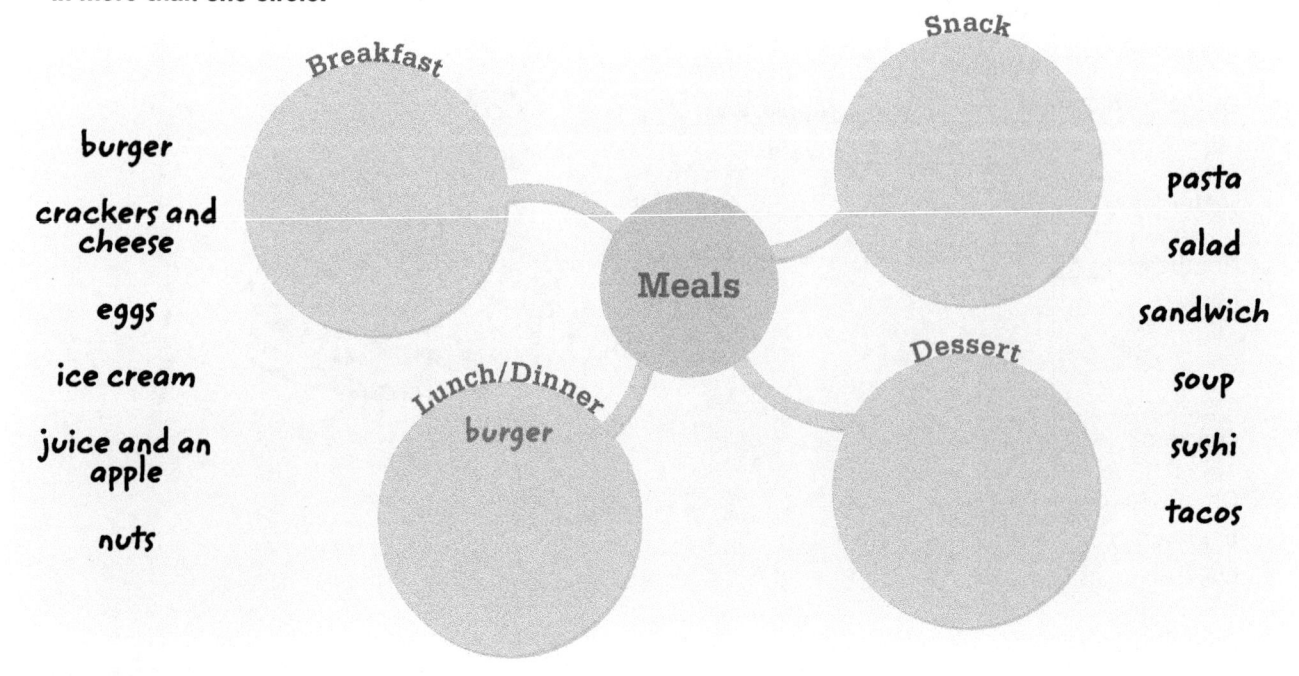

burger
crackers and cheese
eggs
ice cream
juice and an apple
nuts

Breakfast

Snack

Meals

Lunch/Dinner
burger

Dessert

pasta
salad
sandwich
soup
sushi
tacos

38 | Unit 6

GRAMMAR *there is/are* with *much, many,* and *a lot of*

1 Circle the correct words.

1. *There is a* + **singular** / **plural** countable noun.
2. *There is some* + **countable** / **uncountable** noun.
3. *There are some* + **singular** / **plural** countable noun.
4. *There isn't* **some** / **any** + noun.
5. *There aren't* **some** / **any** + noun.

2 Correct the sentences.

1. There ~~are any~~ cheese in the refrigerator. *is some*
2. Are there some milk?
3. There isn't an oranges.
4. There are any bananas?
5. Are there some rice?
6. There aren't a pasta.

3 Circle the correct answers.

1. How **many** / **much** bananas are there?
2. How **much** / **many** juice is there?
3. There is **a lot of** / **many** milk on the table.
4. There is **much** / **a lot** of food on my plate.
5. There are **much** / **many** oranges in the basket.
6. There is **many** / **a lot** of water in the pot.

4 Complete the conversation.

A: Do you want a snack?

B: Sure! ¹_____ cake left from yesterday?

A: No, there ²_____ cake, but there ³_____ a lot of cheese.

B: Cheese and crackers sound good. ⁴_____ there ⁵_____ crackers?

A: Oh, no. No crackers, but ⁶_____ bread and a tomato. We could make cheese and tomato sandwiches.

B: Sounds good!

5 Look in the fridge. Answer the questions. Use *some, a lot of, much, an,* and *any*.

1. How much milk is there?
   There isn't much milk.

2. How many apples are there?
   _____

3. How much bread is there?
   _____

4. How much juice is there?
   _____

5. How many carrots are there?
   _____

6. How much cheese is there?
   _____

7. How much cake is there?
   _____

Unit 6 | 39

CONVERSATION   At a café

1 Put the words in the correct order to make questions. Then match the questions with the correct answers.

1. can / get / you / What / I / ?
   What can I get you? — a. Tomato soup. Thank you.

2. Can / get / you / else / anything / I / ?
   _____ — b. Yes. I'd like some orange juice, please.

3. you / of soup / do / want / What / kind / ?
   _____ — c. I'd also like some soup.

4. to drink / Can / you / get / something / I / ?
   _____ — d. Can I have a fish sandwich?

2 Look at the menu. Write sentences or questions for ordering lunch at this café.

MENU

DRINKS
- milk
- juice *changes by the day*
- tea
- coffee
- water

DESSERTS
- chocolate cake
- orange ice cream

SANDWICHES, ETC.
- fish tacos
- chicken and cheese sandwich
- fish sandwich
- lettuce and tomato sandwich

SOUP
- tomato
- potato
- chicken rice
- chili

Ask about our soup of the day.

1. Ask a question about the soup of the day.
   What is the soup of the day?

2. Order a sandwich. Use _I'd like_.
   _____

3. Ask a question about juice. Use _kinds of_.
   _____

4. Order soup. Use _Can I have_.
   _____

5. Ask a question about the chili. Use _have meat_.
   _____

6. Order a sandwich. Make your own kind.
   _____

40 | Unit 6

READING TO WRITE

1 Complete the invitation with the correct question words.

Invitation
Elena's Birthday Party

The Rainbow Café
25 Prospect Road • Mason, Ohio

Elena's soccer teammates   Saturday, April 12 • Noon

Who   What   When   Where

2 Circle four more time connectors.

(Before) dinner, I do my homework. While I eat dinner, I talk to my family about my day. After dinner, I have dessert. Then I watch soccer on TV before I go to bed.

3 Put the events in order. Then write a paragraph about a basketball game. Use time connectors.

_____ Celebrate with my teammates

_____ Make 10 points

____1___ Put on my basketball clothes

_____ Walk home

_____ Walk to the game

_____ Win the game

Before I walk to the game, I put on my basketball clothes.

_____
_____
_____
_____
_____

REVIEW UNITS 5-6

1 Put the words in the correct columns.

art room	fish	math
cafeteria	history	meat
cheese	ICT	sandwich
civics	library	science lab
English	main office	sushi

School places	School subjects	Foods

2 Write four uncountable foods from Exercise 1.

1. _____
2. _____
3. _____
4. _____

3 Complete the paragraph with foods you eat.

I sometimes have ¹_____ for breakfast. I usually have ²_____ for lunch. I often drink ³_____ with my lunch. I don't like ⁴_____ so I never have it for a snack. I usually have ⁵_____ or ⁶_____ for a snack. For dinner, I often have ⁷_____ with ⁸_____. And for dessert I have ⁹_____.

4 Complete the sentences with *is there*, *are there*, *there is*, or *there are*. Then match the questions with the answers.

1. _____ any milk in the fridge? _____
    a. _____ a lot of sushi.

2. _____ any potatoes in the kitchen? _____
    b. Yes, there is.

3. How much sushi _____? _____
    c. _____ three carrots.

4. How many carrots _____? _____
    d. Yes, there are.

5 Complete the conversation.

| a lot of |
| any |
| Are there |
| How many |
| many |
| much |
| there are |
| there is |

Alex: Let's make a salad.

Gina: Good idea! ¹_____ any vegetables?

Alex: Yes, ²_____. We have carrots.

Gina: ³_____ tomatoes are there?

Alex: There aren't ⁴_____ – just two. But they're very big.

Gina: How ⁵_____ cheese is there?

Alex: There's ⁶_____ cheese.

Gina: Is there ⁷_____ soup to go with our salad?

Alex: Yes, ⁸_____ a lot of potato soup.

6 Circle the correct words.

1. **Josh:** **Can / Do** you like **playing / doing** kung fu?
   Nick: Yes, I love **them / it**.
2. **Jake:** What sports **can / do** you and **your / you** brother like?
   Howard: **Us / We** like playing basketball, but **us / we** don't play that well.
3. **Sally:** **We / Us** need help with **our / us** homework.
   Bettina: I'm sure **me / my** older sister **may / can** help.
4. **Jack:** **Can / Do** you give **we / us** a ride to the park to go skateboarding?
   Brooke: Yes, sure. **I / Me** can take **us / you**.
5. **Terry:** **You / We** can play baseball better than **me / it**.
   Jackson: Thanks, Terry. **I / You** are nice to say that!

7 Put the words in the correct order to ask for and give permission.

1. I / go / the / main office / to / Can / ?
   _____
2. You / go / may / class / during / not / .
   _____
3. I / to / have / give / an / them / important / letter / .
   _____
4. you / go / on your way / class / to / next / your / Can / ?
   _____
5. no / problem / Sure, /.
   _____

8 Match the answers to the questions.

a. Yes, that's right, thank you.
b. A steak salad.
c. I'd like a salad, please.
d. Just water, please.
e. Oh yes, some carrot soup, too.

A: What can I get you?
B: 1_____
A: What kind of salad do you want?
B: 2_____
A: Anything else?
B: 3_____
A: Anything to drink?
B: 4_____
A: OK. That's a steak salad, carrot soup, and water.
B: 5_____

7 Animal World

VOCABULARY Animals

1 Circle 17 more animals.

spider sheep polar bear bird zebra giraffe elephant monkey tiger fish horse pig gorilla shark dog cat cow frog

2 Circle the correct answers.

1. Which animal DOESN'T live in water?
   a. fish   b. frog   c. giraffe
2. Which animal DOESN'T live on a farm?
   a. cow   b. monkey   c. horse
3. Which animal DOESN'T eat plants?
   a. lion   b. cow   c. sheep
4. Which animal DOESN'T eat meat?
   a. dog   b. tiger   c. cow

3 Choose five animals from Exercise 1. Write a sentence about each animal. Use words from the box.

| eat bugs | eat plants | fly |
| live in Africa | swim | |

1. _____ Polar bears can't fly. _____
2. _____
3. _____
4. _____
5. _____
6. _____

4 Complete the sentences with your own ideas.

1. My favorite water animal is the __frog__ because __it can jump high__.
2. My favorite farm animal is the _____ because _____.
3. I love _____ because _____.
4. I don't like _____ because _____.
5. I want to learn more about _____ because _____.

44 | Unit 7

GRAMMAR Present continuous

1 **Look at Sam's photos from the zoo. Correct the sentences with the present continuous of the verbs. Use contractions.**

eat	play	stand
look	~~sleep~~	swim

1. The lions are fighting.
   The lions aren't fighting. They're sleeping.

2. The baby gorilla is eating its lunch in the tree.
   _____
   _____

3. I'm looking at a frog.
   _____
   _____

4. The monkeys are drinking.
   _____
   _____

5. The polar bears are sleeping.
   _____
   _____

6. He's sitting next to an elephant.
   _____
   _____

2 **Complete the conversation with the present continuous form of the verbs. Use contractions.**

Kari: Are these your photos from Safari Park?

Rose: Yes. Look. Here are the tigers. They ¹ _'re watching_ (watch) us, but they ² _____ (not do) anything. In this photo, the baby tigers ³ _____ (fight)! Aren't they cute?

Kari: ⁴ _____ (the monkey hide)?

Rose: No, he ⁵ _____ (play)!

Kari: Oh, right!

Rose: And here, I ⁶ _____ (look) at a snake.

Kari: Oooh! What ⁷ _____ (your mom do)?

Rose: She ⁸ _____ (run) away!

3 **Write questions in the present continuous. Answer the questions for you. Use contractions.**

1. What / you / study / in science?
   What are you studying in science?
   I'm studying the weather.

2. What / after-school activities / you / do?
   _____
   _____

3. What / you / do / in gym class?
   _____
   _____

4. What / you / read / in English?
   _____
   _____

VOCABULARY Action verbs

1 Find six more action verbs.

S	W	I	N	G	I	N	G	H
K	Z	L	H	C	D	B	U	I
S	W	I	M	M	I	N	G	D
R	Y	H	Q	A	T	U	D	I
Z	H	G	Y	W	H	W	K	N
C	I	Z	F	L	Y	I	N	G
M	E	(H	U	N	T	I	N	G)
F	I	G	H	T	I	N	G	G
Z	P	J	U	M	P	I	N	G

2 Complete the sentences. Use the action words from Exercise 1.

1. I am ____*jumping*____ out of the tree at the moment.
2. The tiger is _____ for food right now.
3. At the moment, the boy is _____ in the lake.
4. Tom is _____ in an airplane right now.
5. Now, Sheila is _____ on the swings on the playground.
6. Why are you _____ behind the tree?
7. The baby lions aren't _____. They're playing.

3. How do these animals travel? Match the animals to the verbs.

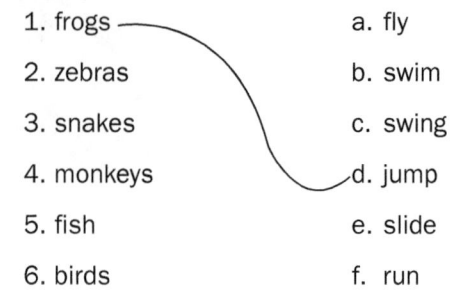

1. frogs   a. fly
2. zebras   b. swim
3. snakes   c. swing
4. monkeys   d. jump
5. fish   e. slide
6. birds   f. run

4 Look at the pictures. Correct the sentences.

1. The boy is ~~hunting~~. *swimming*
2. The girl is flying.
3. The boys are hiding.
4. The girls are jumping.
5. The birds are eating.

GRAMMAR Simple present vs. present continuous

1 Complete the rules with *simple present* or *present continuous*.

1. To talk about facts, habits, and routines, we use the _____.

2. To talk about an action that is happening now, we use the _____.

3. We use *always*, *usually*, *sometimes*, and *never* with the _____.

4. We use *now* and *at the moment* with the _____.

2 Circle the correct forms of the verbs.

Suncoast Seabird Sanctuary

Hi, my name is Sue. Right now, I ¹**work** / **('m working)** at the Suncoast Seabird Sanctuary during my school vacation. It's a great job! About 10,000 birds ²**come** / **are coming** here each year. At the moment, we ³**look** / **'re looking** after more than one hundred birds! Suncoast is near the sea, so we have a lot of sea birds. This is my favorite bird, Billy. He has a bad wing, so the vet ⁴**looks** / **is looking** at him now. I ⁵**feed** / **am feeding** Billy fish. A lot of people ⁶**visit** / **are visiting** the sanctuary every year, especially in the summer. We always ⁷**explain** / **are explaining** what we do to help the birds. We're open every day. Come and visit us!

3 Write the correct forms of the verbs.

swim

1. In this photo, three dolphins _____ next to our boat!

2. Dolphins _____ very fast, up to 25 miles an hour.

lie

3. Cows usually _____ down in the same direction when it rains.

4. Look! The cows in that field _____ down.

eat

5. Large spiders _____ frogs and other small animals.

6. Oh! The cat _____ our dinner.

play

7. Today, _____ with my uncle's dog, Patch.

8. I always _____ with Patch on the weekend.

4 Complete the sentences with the simple present or present continuous of the verbs and your own ideas.

1. On the weekend, I usually ___*do my homework*___ . (do)

2. At the moment, I _____. (read)

3. My friends and I sometimes _____. (go)

4. Right this minute, I _____.

Unit 7 | **47**

CONVERSATION: Asking for and giving directions

1 Put the words in order to make sentences.

1. do / get / I / How / to / bird exhibit / the / ?

   How do I get to the bird exhibit?

2. down / Walk / hall / the / your / left / to / .

   _____

3. on / Is / it / the / floor / second / ?

   _____

4. Yes, it is. / a / Take / at / stairs / top / right / the / the / of / .

   _____

5. Then turn left. / down / on / the hall / the right / It's / .

   _____

2 Help the boys from Exercise 1 find the polar bear exhibit. Complete the sentences to give them directions.

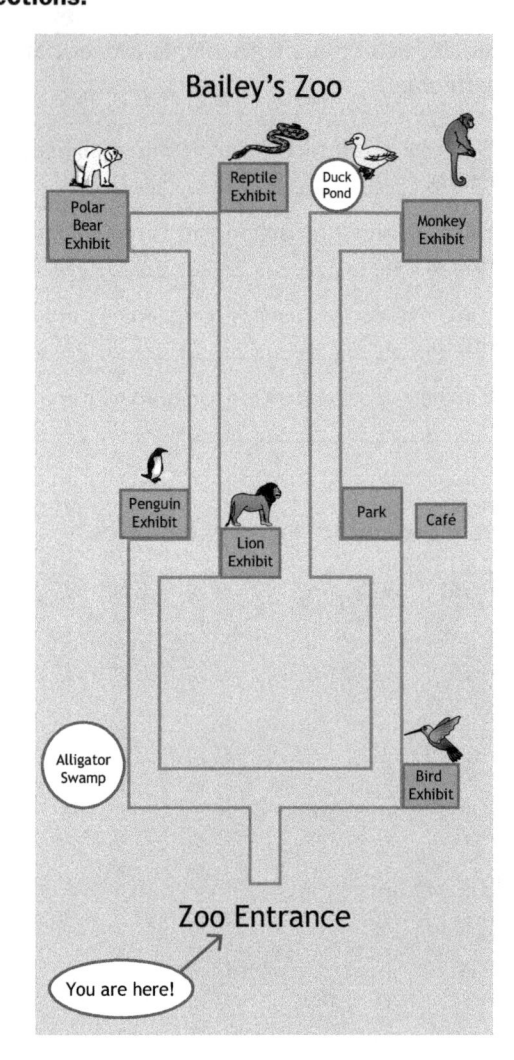

1. *Go into the zoo entrance and take a left.*
2. Take a right at the _____.
3. _____ at the penguin exhibit.
4. Take a left at the _____.
5. At the reptile exhibit, _____.
6. The polar bear exhibit is _____.

3 Now write directions from the zoo entrance to the monkey exhibit. Write six sentences.

1. _____
2. _____
3. _____
4. _____
5. _____
6. _____

READING TO WRITE

1 Complete the word web with the information.

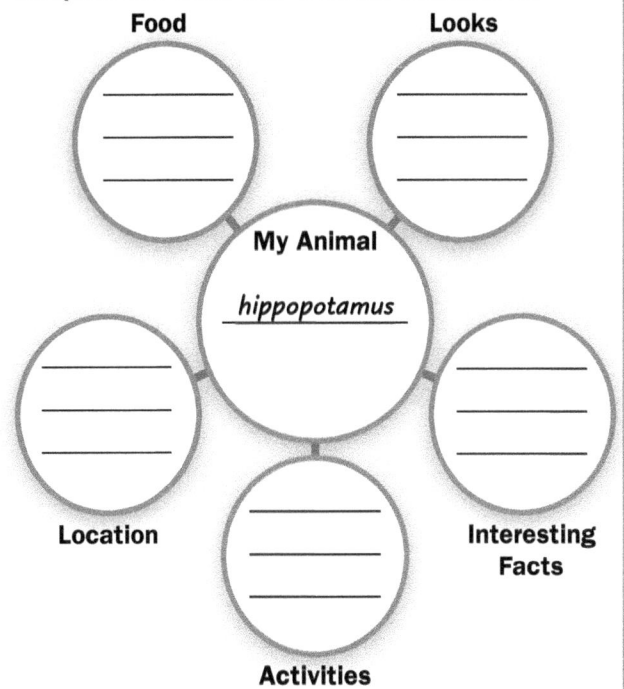

- Food
- Looks
- My Animal: *hippopotamus*
- Location
- Activities
- Interesting Facts

huge head
Africa
~~hippopotamus~~
lives in warm rivers and lakes
weighs up to 7,000 pounds
short neck
can run faster than a person
at night, climbs out of water and eats grass
long, round body
34 to 36 huge teeth
sleeps standing up in water during the day
different kinds of fish clean different parts of a hippo's body
strong, short legs

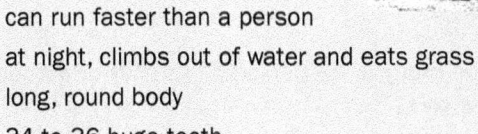

2 Put the words in order to make sentences about hippos. Then circle the adjectives.

1. large / are / Hippos / animals / very / .
   Hippos are very (large) animals.

2. have / They / legs / strong / .
   _____

3. have / Hippos / teeth / huge / .
   _____

4. are / fast / Hippos / very / .
   _____

5. sleep / rivers / in / They / warm / .
   _____

3 Read the facts about polar bears. Then read the sentences. Are the sentences true (*T*) or false (*F*)?

FACTS ABOUT POLAR BEARS

live in the Arctic
hunt seals
have thick fur
paws up to 12 inches across
ears small and round
short tails
adult males weigh up to 1,200 pounds
adult females weigh up to 650 pounds

1. Polar bears live all over the world. ___F___
2. Polar bears have short tails and small, round ears. _____
3. Polar bears have large paws. _____
4. Male and female polar bears weigh the same. _____
5. Polar bears have very little fur. _____

8 City Life

VOCABULARY Places in town

1. Put the letters in the correct order to make places in town. Then match the words with the correct pictures.

   a.  1. MSKETUPRARE
      supermarket

   b. 2. TKASE ARPK
      _____

   c. 3. EFISNTS TECNRE
      _____

   d. 4. WLBOING LEYAL
      _____

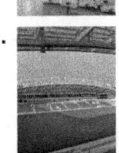

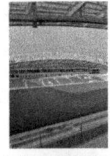

   e. 5. IMUSTAD
      _____

   f. 6. MEUSUM
      _____

   g. 7. VIEMO EATHTER
      _____

   h. 8. AMLL
      _____

   i. 9. ARKMTE
      _____

   j. 10. RKAP
      _____

2. Put the places in town from Exercise 1 in the correct columns. Some places go in more than one column. Add other places in your town.

Indoor places	Outdoor places	Places to have fun	Places to exercise
supermarket			

3. Where can you do these things? Write places from Exercise 1.

   1. watch a football game or see a concert
      ____stadium____

   2. buy some new jeans (2 places)
      _____ _____

   3. go swimming or take a karate class
      _____

   4. go on a field trip to learn about history
      _____

   5. buy food (2 places)
      _____ _____

4 Complete the sentences with your own information.

1. I love going to _the mall. The clothes are great!_
2. I like going to _____
3. I never go to _____
4. On the weekend, I sometimes go to _____
5. I sometimes go to _____ in another town.

GRAMMAR Simple past of *be* and *there was/were*

1 Circle the correct words.

1. I/He/She/It **was / were** there.
2. You/We/They **was / were** there.
3. He **wasn't / weren't** there.
4. **Was you / Were you** there?

2 Read the email. Circle the correct forms of *be*.

Hey Sam,

Yesterday, my dad and I went to the football stadium to see the Mavericks play the Chargers, but it ¹ **wasn't / weren't** much fun. My favorite team, the Chargers, lost by a lot. It ² **was / were** hard to watch my team lose. They ³ **wasn't / weren't** nearly as good as the other team. My team ⁴ **wasn't / weren't** playing well. My dad and I ⁵ **wasn't / weren't** happy that they lost so badly.

⁶ **Was / Were** you watching the game on TV? Did you think it ⁷ **was / were** fun? What's your favorite team this year? I know last year it ⁸ **was / were** the Mavericks.

Your friend,
Tyler

3 Complete the sentences with the correct forms of *there was* and *there were*.

1. In 2013, __there were__ many tourists in our town because of the new museum and stadium.
2. Before the new museum and stadium opened, _____ many people who visited here.
3. Last week _____ an exhibit at the museum. _____ a lot of people there to meet a famous artist.
4. _____ an important game at the stadium last Saturday?
5. The stadium was full. _____ any seats left.

4 Complete the questions with *was* or *were*. Then answer the questions.

1. Where __were__ you yesterday afternoon at three o'clock?
   I was at home doing my homework.
2. What _____ your favorite TV show when you _____ younger?
   _____
3. How old _____ you in 2010?
   _____
4. How many students _____ there in your class last year?
   _____
5. _____ you out of school yesterday?
   _____
6. _____ there a test yesterday?
   _____

VOCABULARY Transportation places and prepositions of place

1 Label the places in the city. Correct the sentences to match the map.

1. The subway station is across the street from the market.

   The subway station is across the street from Tom's Restaurant.

2. The bus stop is behind the movie theater.
   _____

3. The girl is in front of the subway station.
   _____

4. The boy is behind the market.
   _____

5. The market is across the street from Carl's Coffee Café and the movie theater.
   _____

6. The woman is behind Tom's restaurant.
   _____

7. The bus station is behind the parking lot.
   _____

8. Sally's Shoe Shop is next to Mel's Market.
   _____

2 Complete the paragraph.

airport	ferry port	~~subway~~	train
bus stop	parking lot	taxi	

My family lives in the city. My mom works downtown. She takes an underground train called a ¹ _____subway_____. My dad works outside the city. He takes a ² _____, too, but it's not underground. He leaves his car in the ³ _____ at the station. I wait for the bus at the ⁴ _____ each morning to go to school.

Every year, we fly to Washington to visit my grandparents. We don't have a car, so we ride in a ⁵ _____ to the ⁶ _____ to get on the plane. My grandparents live on an island called Mercer Island. After we get off the plane, we go to the ⁷ _____ to get a boat to the island.

GRAMMAR Simple past with regular and irregular verbs

1 Write the simple past forms of the regular verbs.

1. watch ____watched____
2. shop _____
3. wait _____
4. study _____
5. play _____
6. visit _____
7. like _____

2 Complete the sentences with the simple past form of the verbs.

1. Roman children ____played____ (play) board games.
2. We _____ (listen) to the concert at the stadium.
3. Katia and her friends _____ (wait) for the bus.
4. My family _____ (live) in the city last year.
5. They _____ (shop) at the mall.
6. We _____ (stay) at the bowling alley after 9:00 p.m.

3 Rewrite the sentences to make them negative. Use contractions.

1. My family watched the football game on TV.
   My family didn't watch the football game on TV.
2. They visited the museum on their vacation.
   _____
3. We shopped at the mall for new shoes.
   _____
4. Jenna waited for her mom at the restaurant.
   _____
5. I studied for the test last night.
   _____
6. My brother played tennis in the park.
   _____

4 Write the simple past form of the irregular verbs.

1. see ____saw____
2. go _____
3. speak _____
4. fly _____
5. buy _____
6. take _____
7. understand _____

5 Complete the sentences with the correct form of the verbs.

do

1. Did you _____ anything fun at the park?
2. Yes, we _____. There were a lot of other kids to play with.

speak

3. Did you _____ in front of the class last week?
4. Yes, I _____ in front of all my classmates.

eat

5. Did you _____ at that new restaurant in the mall?
6. Yes, I _____ there. The food was great!

go

7. Did you _____ to the skate park three days ago?
8. No, I _____ to the mall.

CONVERSATION That sounds fun!

1 Complete the conversation.

Speech bubble (left): How was your vacation Sally?
Speech bubble (right): It was great!

Where did you go on vacation?	Can you believe it	Did you know that
Guess what	And that's not all	What else did you do
What	sounds fun	so cool

Katie: ¹ _Where did you go on vacation?_

Sally: My family and I went to Boston. We went to the Museum of Science and to Quincy Market.

Katie: Wow! That ² _____.

Sally: Yeah. ³ _____.

Katie: ⁴ _____?

Sally: Well, we did something really awesome! ⁵ _____ we did.

Katie: I don't know. ⁶ _____?

Sally: We went to the Top of the Hub Restaurant. It's 52 floors high!

Katie: That's ⁷ _____!

Sally: And after dinner we took a walk. ⁸ _____ it has a skywalk?
⁹ _____? We could see all of Boston from up there!

2 Write four more words to describe an exciting time.

1. _amazing_
2. _____
3. _____
4. _____
5. _____

READING TO WRITE

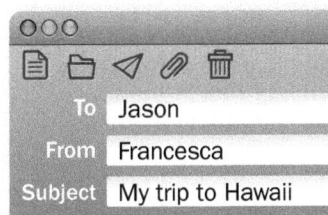

To: Jason
From: Francesca
Subject: My trip to Hawaii

Hi Jason,

How was your vacation? My trip to Hawaii was great! My family and I landed at the airport on the "Big Island." It is about the size of the state of Connecticut. The state of Hawaii has hundreds of islands, but there are eight big islands. Hawaii became the last state of the United States in 1950. It's also the only state made up of islands! And the only state not located in the Americas. It is in Polynesia in the central Pacific Ocean.

We saw amazing waterfalls and went to Hawaii Volcanoes National Park and saw the active volcano, Kilauea. We went swimming and surfing, too. The beaches are beautiful!

On our last night, we went to a *luau*, a Hawaiian party. We ate *poi*, a kind of plant, and also some delicious fish. We listened to Hawaiian music and watched a dance called the *hula*, too.

I didn't want to come home! I can't wait to hear about your vacation!

Your friend,

Francesca

1 Read Francesca's email. Complete the word web.

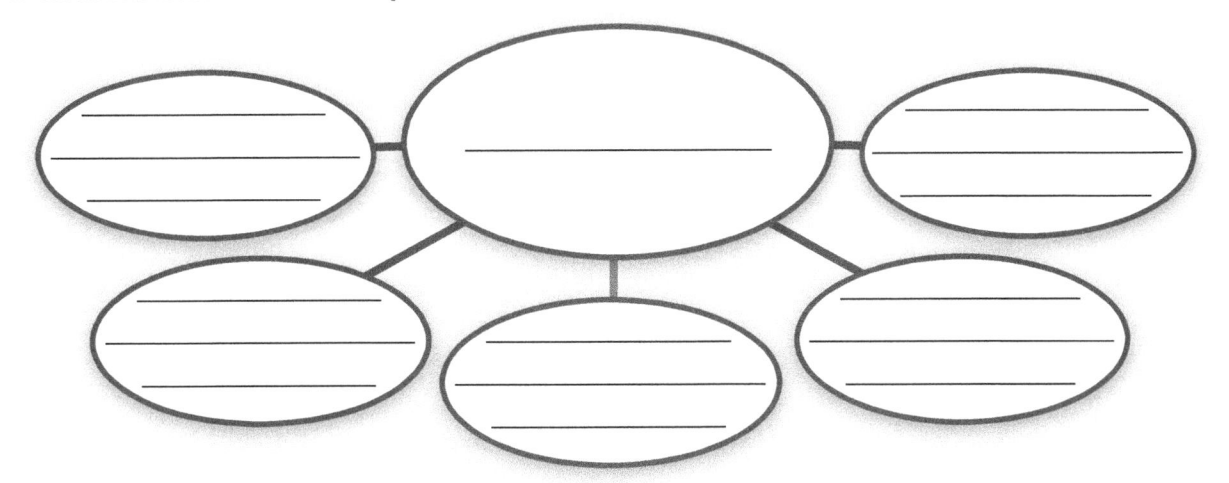

2 Circle examples of *also* and *too* in Francesca's email.

3 Rewrite the sentences using *too* or *also*.

1. My brother and I flew to Chicago this summer. (New York / too)
   We flew to New York, too.

2. I went to the zoo yesterday. (beach / also)
   _____

3. Sally is studying for her math test. (history test / too)
   _____

4. Jim and Michael are going to ride their bikes. (go swimming / too)
   _____

REVIEW UNITS 7–8

1 Match the descriptions to the correct pictures. Then write the names of the places.

1. a place to wait for a taxi _____
   _____

2. a place to buy groceries _____
   _____

3. an animal that lives on a farm _____
   _____

4. a place to learn about art and history _____
   _____

5. an animal with a very long neck _____
   _____

6. a place to watch a concert _____
   _____

7. a place to take a boat _____
   _____

8. a place to lift weights _____
   _____

9. an animal that lives in the Arctic _____
   _____

10. a place to leave a car _____
    _____

2 Complete the sentences with the simple present, present continuous, or simple past of the verbs.

1. I _____ (go) to the bus station yesterday.

2. I usually _____ (take) a taxi to the airport.

3. Tom and Lila _____ (visit) the museum now.

4. She _____ (speak) to her brother last night at the train station.

5. Tim always _____ (ride) a bus to work.

6. Sera and Fran _____ (eat) lunch at the moment.

3 Circle the correct answers.

1. _____ a lot of birds flying over the lake yesterday.
   a. There are   b. There were

2. No, the tiger _____ in the jungle right now.
   a. isn't hunting   b. didn't hunt

3. _____ ducks at the pond today?
   a. Are there   b. There were

4. Petra, Angkor, and Tanis _____ small towns in the past.
   a. were   b. are

5. I _____ Hawaii with my family last winter.
   a. visited   b. is visiting

6. _____ many tourists there when we went.
   a. There wasn't   b. There weren't

7. I _____ to Paris a few years ago.
   a. am flying   b. flew

8. My parents usually _____ home on Saturdays.
   a. stay   b. are staying

4 Complete the sentences with the correct forms of the verbs. Write *simple present*, *present continuous*, or *simple past*.

| fight | hunt | swim |
| hide | ~~jump~~ | playing |

1. The frogs __*are jumping*__ from rock to rock now.
   ____*present continuous*____

2. The tigers _____ in the jungle last night for their meal. _____

56 | Review 4

3. At the moment, those angry cats _____ with each other. _____

4. Sharks always _____ in the sea. _____

5. The spiders _____ inside the tree right now. _____

6. The cute puppies _____ with a ball yesterday. _____

5 Put the words in the correct order to ask for and give directions.

1. can / I / Where / find / the / ferry port / ?

   _____

2. on the way / to / fish market / the / It's / .

   _____

3. the corner / Go up / the stairs / and / turn right / at / .

   _____

4. Take a / bus stop / in front of / the / left / .

   _____

5. Turn right / at / mall / the / and / then / straight / go / .

   _____

6 Answer the questions about your favorite animal. Write complete sentences.

1. What is your favorite animal?

   _____

2. Where does it live?

   _____

3. What does it look like?

   _____

4. What does it eat?

   _____

7 Answer the questions about your favorite place. Write complete sentences.

1. What is your favorite place?

   _____

2. Where is it?

   _____

3. What does it look like?

   _____

4. What do you like to do there?

   _____

8 Complete the conversation.

I can't wait to see them
I can't wait to see you
That sounds so beautiful
What fun things did you do there
What else did you do

Janet: Hello?

Stella: Hi, Janet! It's Stella. How are you? Guess what! Last month, I flew to Paris with my mom. What an amazing vacation!

Janet: ¹_____?

Stella: We saw the Mona Lisa in the Louvre Museum, and we went to the Eiffel Tower.

Janet: ²_____?

Stella: We also took a boat ride down the Seine at night and saw Paris with all its lights!

Janet: ³_____!

Stella: It was. We also ate a lot of delicious food, and I bought some cool clothes at a street market. I put my photos online so you and my other friends can see my amazing trip.

Janet: ⁴_____!

Stella: We had a fantastic time. I have a lot more to tell you. And I want to hear about your vacation, too!

Janet: ⁵_____! When can we get together?

Review 4 | 57

9 Fun and Games

VOCABULARY Sports and activities

1 Use the pictures to complete the crossword.

Down

Across

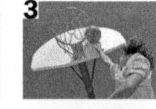

2 Complete the word web with the sports from Exercise 1.

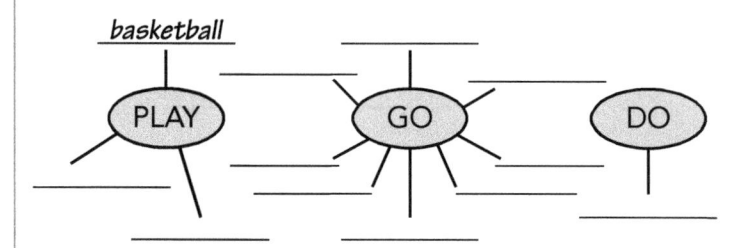

basketball

PLAY   GO   DO

3 Complete the paragraph with the sports words from Exercise 1.

I love water sports! I go ¹ _swimming_ in the pool a lot. But I don't live near the ocean, so I don't go ² _____ or ³ _____. I don't like snow, so I don't go ⁴ _____ or ⁵ _____. I like sports you play with teams. I like playing ⁶ _____, ⁷ _____, and ⁸ _____. I just started doing ⁹ _____. It's fun, but I'm not very good yet. I'm only a white belt. I got a new bike for my birthday, so now my favorite thing to do is to go ¹⁰ _____ in the park with my friends. Sometimes I also go ¹¹ _____ in the park. On rainy days, I go ¹² _____.

4 Which sports do you like? Write at least three sentences. Use the ideas below or your own ideas.

boring	easy for me
dangerous	fun
difficult for me	scary

1. _I think bowling is fun, but it is difficult for me._
2. _____
3. _____
4. _____

58 | Unit 9

GRAMMAR Simple past yes/no questions and short answers

1 Complete the text with the negative simple past form of the verbs.

buy	go
eat	see
~~go~~	win

Yesterday was Saturday, so I ¹ ___didn't go___ to school. I got up very late, so I ² _____ any breakfast, just lunch. Then I went shopping, but I ³ _____ anything good, so I ⁴ _____ anything. My parents went bowling last night, but my brother Mike and I ⁵ _____. We stayed home and watched a baseball game on TV. Our team ⁶ _____.

2 Complete the questions about Exercise 1. Then answer the questions with short answers.

1. Q: ___Did you go___ (you / go) to school yesterday?
   A: ___No, I didn't.___

2. Q: _____ (you / get) up very late?
   A: _____

3. Q: _____ (you / eat) any lunch?
   A: _____

4. Q: _____ (you / buy) anything when you went shopping?
   A: _____

5. Q: _____ (your parents / go) bowling last night?
   A: _____

6. Q: _____ (you and Mike / stay) home last night?
   A: _____

7. Q: _____ (you and Mike / watch) soccer on TV?
   A: _____

8. Q: _____ (your team / win) yesterday?
   A: _____

3 Write affirmative (✓) and negative (✗) sentences in the simple past.

1. I (ride) my bike last night. (✗)
   ___I didn't ride my bike last night.___

2. My cousins (go) snowboarding last week. (✓)
   _____

3. Tracy and I (play) volleyball this morning. (✓)
   _____

4. John (watch) a movie yesterday. (✗)
   _____

5. Mary (do) judo last night. (✗)
   _____

6. Harry and I (play) baseball last summer. (✓)
   _____

7. Justin (study) for his test this morning. (✓)
   _____

8. I (speak) to my friend last night. (✗)
   _____

9. He (eat) a big breakfast yesterday. (✗)
   _____

10. Cathy (make) her bed this morning. (✓)
    _____

4 Answer these questions about you.

1. Did you go skiing this year?
   ___No, I didn't.___

2. Did you play basketball last week?
   _____

3. Did you watch TV yesterday?
   _____

4. Did you go bowling last winter?
   _____

Unit 9 | 59

VOCABULARY Clothes

1 Put the letters in order to make clothes words.

1. STTARCKIUT _tracksuit_
2. SEWASRITTH _____
3. STHRIT- _____
4. NTPAS _____
5. OTOBS _____
6. TRIKS _____
7. SKOSC _____
8. DEOHOI _____
9. PAC _____
10. KEJCAT _____
11. EJASN _____
12. TRSHOS _____

2 Circle the words that don't belong.

1. jeans   pants   (boots)
2. sweatshirt T-shirt   socks
3. sneakers   boots   skirt
4. dress   skirt   cap
5. hoodie   sweatshirt   dress
6. T-shirt   socks   sneakers
7. jacket   shorts   hoodie

3 Circle the correct answers.

1. People usually don't wear _____ in very hot weather.
   a. a sweatshirt   b. sneakers   c. shorts

2. Jenna wears _____ to play volleyball.
   a. a jacket   b. shorts   c. boots

3. In the Olympics, runners wear _____ before the race.
   a. tracksuits   b. socks   c. a cap

4. Mary wears _____ to hike.
   a. a skirt   b. boots   c. a dress

5. In the winter, I wear _____ over my shirt.
   a. a cap   b. a jacket   c. socks

4 Read your activities for tomorrow. Plan your clothes. It is very cold in the morning. Later in the day, it is warmer.

6:00 a.m. go running outside	sneakers
8:00 a.m. go to school	
3:00 p.m. play tennis outside	
6:00 p.m. go out to dinner	

GRAMMAR Simple past
Wh- questions

1 Match the questions to the correct answers.

1. Who did you go windsurfing with?
2. Where did you read that?
3. When did you go skiing?
4. How many miles did we ride?
5. How did you get to the store?
6. What did you wear?

a. Yesterday afternoon.
b. Karla and Sammie.
c. In the newspaper.
d. My new jacket.
e. Almost 20.
f. By car.

2 Complete the questions.

1. _____ did you do yesterday?
   We went windsurfing.
2. _____ did you go windsurfing?
   We went to Malibu Beach.
3. _____ did you go?
   We went in the early afternoon.
4. _____ did you get to the beach?
   We went by car.
5. _____ long did you windsurf?
   We windsurfed for a couple of hours.

3 Complete the chart with information from the paragraph.

> Karen and her best friend, Carrie, went to Mount Kemo in New Hampshire yesterday. They went by bus with some people from their ski club. They wore their new ski jackets and ski boots. They got there early in the morning. They skied all morning. At noon they had a big lunch. They were very hungry after so much exercise. After lunch they went snowboarding. They were tired on the way home. They fell asleep on the bus.

What?	went skiing and snowboarding
Who?	
Where?	
How?	
When?	

4 Complete the Wh- questions and about Exercise 3. Answer the questions.

1. Q: _____*What did*_____ Karen and Carrie ____*wear*____?
   A: _____
2. Q: _____ they get there?
   A: _____ early in the morning.
3. Q: _____ they _____ lunch?
   A: _____
4. Q: _____ they _____ after lunch?
   A: _____
5. Q: _____ they _____ asleep?
   A: _____

CONVERSATION   It sounds fantastic!

1 Put the sentences in order to make a conversation.

_1_	**Michael:**	What did you do on vacation, Todd?
___	**Michael:**	Cool! How was that?
___	**Todd:**	I went snowboarding.
___	**Michael:**	Really? That's too bad.
___	**Todd:**	I kept losing the board. I had to run down the mountain after it.
___	**Michael:**	Now, that sounds like fun!
___	**Todd:**	Yeah, but after a while, I learned to stay on and even turn. I loved flying across the snow.
___	**Todd:**	It was really great! At first, I didn't think I could do it. I had a lot of problems.
___	**Michael:**	Why? What happened?

2 Circle the phrases in Exercise 1 that express interest.

3 Match the questions to the answers.

1. Where did you go on vacation?
2. What else did you do?
3. Why? What happened?
4. Cool! How was that?

a. It was amazing flying in a helicopter over the park!
b. I lost my family hiking on one of the trails, but I finally found them.
c. My family and I went to Yosemite National Park in California.
d. We also went skiing.

READING TO WRITE

1 Read Melissa Franklin's biography. Then complete the timeline of important events in her life.

> Melissa "Missy" Franklin was born(in) 1995 in Pasadena, California, and grew up in Centennial, Colorado. She started swimming when she was five years old. In 2009, at age 14, Missy won her first international swim event. In the 2012 Olympics in London, Missy swam in seven different events and won three gold medals. She set the Olympic record in the backstroke and became the fastest woman ever. In 2013, she became a student at the University of California in Berkeley. She swims on the swim team there. She wants to go to the next Olympics.

Missy was born.

| 1995 | 1996 | 2004 | 2005 | 2006 | 2007 | 2008 | 2009 | 2010 | 2011 | 2012 | 2013 | 2014 | 2015 | 2016 | 2017 | 2018 |

2 Circle the prepositions of time and underline the prepositions of place in Melissa Franklin's biography.

3 Read the biography again. Answer the questions. Write complete sentences.

1. When was Melissa Franklin born?
   She was born in 1995.

2. Where was Melissa Franklin born?
   _____

3. When did Melissa Franklin win her first international swim event?
   _____

4. When did Melissa Franklin swim in the London Olympics?
   _____

5. What did Melissa Franklin set a record in at the 2012 Olympics?
   _____

6. Where does Melissa Franklin go to school?
   _____

10 Vacation: Here and There

VOCABULARY Weather, months, and seasons

1 Find seven more weather words.

S	T	O	R	M	Y	P	W	D
F	O	G	G	Y	F	H	C	Z
I	H	A	L	S	U	N	N	Y
C	R	A	I	N	Y	O	O	B
Y	P	S	N	O	W	Y	J	H
F	N	G	W	I	N	D	Y	Q
F	W	S	P	X	D	O	H	C
W	I	C	L	O	U	D	Y	S
T	M	X	A	O	X	H	P	I

2 Complete the sentences. Use the words from Exercise 1.

Hello! Here is today's world weather:

1. At the moment in Kingston, Jamaica, it's the ____*rainy*____ season. Today there's a lot of rain, and it's very ____*stormy*____.

2. In London today, the weather is 12°C. It's gray and _____, but you don't need your umbrella — it isn't _____.

3. In Ottawa it's cold (–1°C) and very _____. People are making snowmen.

4. Today in San Francisco, it's very _____. You can't see anything, so drive carefully.

5. In Helsinki, it's –2°C today. It's cold and _____, so it's a good day to skate!

6. In Rio de Janeiro today it's beach weather. It's hot (28°C) and _____.

3 Circle the correct answers.

Jim lives in Connecticut, where there are four seasons. In the winter months, ¹_____, it's cold and ²_____. He likes to ski and ³_____. In the spring, ⁴_____, it gets warm and ⁵_____. Jim plays on the ⁶_____ team at school. In the summer months, ⁷_____, it's hot and ⁸_____. Jim's favorite summer activities are swimming and playing ⁹_____. But Jim's favorite season is fall, ¹⁰_____. It's beginning to get ¹¹_____, but there are many beautiful, sunny days. He plays ¹²_____ in fall.

1. ⓐ December–February
   b. March–May
   c. June–August
2. a. hot   b. warm   c. snowy
3. a. windsurf   b. snowboard   c. swim
4. a. June–August
   b. March–May
   c. September–November
5. a. windy   b. snowy   c. icy
6. a. snowboarding b. baseball   c. skiing

64 | Unit 10

7. a. March–May
   b. June–August
   c. September–November
8. a. sunny   b. snowy   c. cold
9. a. tennis   b. kung fu   c. windsurfing
10. a. March–May
    b. June–August
    c. September–November
11. a. warm   b. cold   c. snowy
12. a. football   b. judo   c. bowling

GRAMMAR be going to

1 Circle the correct words.

1. **He's going to buy / He buys** a camera tomorrow.
2. We **are going to eat / eat** dinner at seven o'clock every night.
3. A: **Are you going to watch / Do you watch** TV tonight?
   B: Yes, **I'm going / I am**.

2 Look at the pictures. What are the people going to do? Complete the sentences with *be going to*.

Amanda

Cristina and me

Me

Lucas

Alicia and Robin

You and your family

1. _Lucas is going to_ learn to ride a horse.
2. _____ be famous movie stars.
3. _____ climb Mount Everest.
4. _____ buy a laptop.
5. _____ live in the country.
6. _____ travel around the world.

3 Complete the sentences. Use *be going to*.

1. What _are you going to do_ (do) now that you finished your homework?
2. When _____ you _____ (visit) your parents?
3. I think my brother _____ (buy) a new MP3 player.
4. I _____ (take) a shower after I exercise.
5. We _____ (not tell) you that!

4 Read the questions. Write "No" answers. Use *be going to* and the activities. Use contractions.

1. Are you going to study for your history test tonight? (study for your French test)

   No, I'm not. I'm going to study for my French test tonight.

2. Are Sally and Missy going to go swimming tomorrow? (play tennis)

   _____

3. Is Paula going to go bowling Saturday? (go windsurfing)

   _____

4. Is Ralph going to visit his grandparents this weekend? (visit his cousins)

   _____

5. Are you going to go snowboarding during vacation? (go skiing)

   _____

VOCABULARY Landforms

1 Write the name of each landform under its picture.

1. an _____ 
2. a _____
3. a _____ 
4. a _____
5. a _____ 
6. a _____
7. a _____ 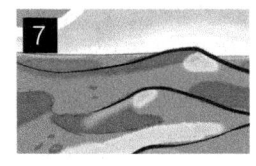
8. a _____ 
9. a _____

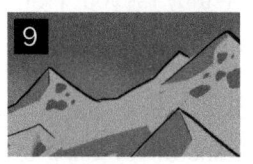

2 Write the landforms in Exercise 1 in the correct columns.

Bodies of water	Bodies of land
ocean	

3 Circle the word that doesn't belong.

1. mountain   lake   hill
2. jungle   lake   ocean
3. forest   jungle   river
4. ocean   desert   beach

4 Complete the sentences. Use the words in the box. There are some extra words.

| beach | jungle | ~~mountain~~ | river |
| desert | lake | ocean | |

1. We got a lot of exercise hiking up and down the ____mountain____ .
2. We went down the _____ in a boat.
3. A tiger is an animal that lives in the _____.
4. We made a castle in the sand at the _____.
5. The Atlantic is an _____, and so is the Pacific.

GRAMMAR Superlatives

1 Complete the rules and write the superlative forms of the adjectives.

1. For most adjectives with one syllable, add _____-est_____ .

   long → ____longest____

2. For most adjectives with two or more syllables, add _____.

   popular → _____

3. For most adjectives ending in consonant + -y, change the ending to _____.

   rainy → _____

4. Some adjectives are irregular:

   good → _____

   bad → _____

66 | Unit 10

2 Write the comparative and superlative forms of the adjectives.

	Comparative	Superlative
tall	*taller*	*tallest*
colorful		
good		
bad		
important		
icy		
beautiful		
popular		

3 Read the information about deserts. Complete the sentences. Use information from the chart.

	Size	Average rainfall	Average temperature
Sahara Desert	3,600,000 sq. miles (9,323,957 sq. km)	3 inches (7.62 cm)	High: 100°F (38°C) Low: 50°F (10°C)
Gobi Desert	500,000 sq. miles (1,294,994 sq. km)	7.6 inches (19.4 cm)	High: 66°F (19°C) Low: 2°F (-17°C)
Arctic Desert	5,405,432 sq. miles (14,000,005 sq. km)	20 inches (51 cm)	High: 50°F (10°C) Low: -32°F (-36°C)
Kalahari Desert	220,000 sq. miles (569,797 sq. km)	2 inches (5.08 cm)	High: 104° F (40°C) Low: 77°F (25°C)

1. The Arctic Desert is the ____*biggest*____ desert.

   It is ____*bigger*____ than the Sahara Desert.

2. The Kalahari is the _____ desert.

   It is _____ than the Gobi Desert.

3. The Arctic gets the _____ rainfall.

   It is the _____ desert.

4. The Kalahari gets the _____ rainfall.

   It is the _____ desert.

5. The Arctic Desert has the _____ temperature. It is much _____ than the Kalahari Desert.

6. The Sahara has the _____ temperature. It is much _____ than the Arctic Desert.

4 Look at the pictures. Write four more sentences using comparative and superlative adjectives.

parrot

hippo

dolphin

rabbit

goat

1. ____*The rabbit has the longest ears.*____
2. _____
3. _____
4. _____
5. _____

5 Answer these questions with your own information. Use superlative adjectives.

1. The _____ (old) person in my family is my _____.

2. The _____ (young) person in my family is _____.

3. The _____ (funny) movie I've ever seen is _____.

4. The _____ (pretty) actress is _____.

5. The _____ (popular) food at my house is _____.

6. The _____ (intelligent) person in my family is _____.

Unit 10 | **67**

CONVERSATION — Making suggestions

1 Put the sentences in order to make a conversation. Write the numbers. Then read the conversation again and circle the suggestions.

_____	**Debbie:**	No. It's too cold to swim. We can go on the roller coaster instead.
_____	**Tania:**	Good plan! But why don't we get something to eat first?
_____	**Tania:**	I don't know. Roller coasters are really scary. What about going windsurfing?
__1__	**Tania:**	Let's go swimming!
_____	**Tania:**	Me too. We can eat and then go windsurfing. It's going to be a wonderful day!
_____	**Debbie:**	Good idea. I'm really hungry!
_____	**Debbie:**	Hmm . . . It's windy today, so it's a good day for it. OK. Let's do that!

2 Complete the conversation with your own ideas. Use the phrases in the box.

how about	we can
let's	why don't we

1. **A:** Let's go swimming.
   B: It's too cold.
   A: _____Let's go to the movies._____
2. **A:** Let's have lunch.
   B: I'm not hungry.
   A: _____
3. **A:** How about riding our bikes?
   B: I'm tired.
   A: _____
4. **A:** Why don't we go skiing?
   B: There's not much snow.
   A: _____
5. **A:** How about playing tennis?
   B: It's too hot.
   A: _____
6. **A:** Let's go windsurfing.
   B: But, it's not windy.
   A: _____

READING TO WRITE

1 Read the email and complete the chart.

To: jenm@net.cup.org
From: sashap@net.cup.org
Subject: My trip to New York City

Thanks for your email! And thanks for the photos of your vacation. It looks like you had lots of fun.

I'm going to go on vacation the last week in June. I'm going to New York City. I'm going to fly there with my mom, dad, and sister. We're going to stay in a fancy hotel near Central Park. Since it's going to be warm, I'm going to skate and cycle in the park.

We're going to visit Ellis Island and the Statue of Liberty. We're going to see the city from the top of the Empire State Building! And I'm going to see the musical *Matilda*. I can't wait!

I hope everything is good with you. Write me soon.

Your friend,
Sasha

Sasha's Vacation	
1. Where is she going to go?	Sasha is going to go to _____.
2. When is she going to go?	She is going to go the last week in _____.
3. What's the weather going to be like?	It is going to be _____.
4. Who is she going to go with?	Sasha is going to go with her _____, _____, and _____.
5. How is she going to get there?	She is going to _____ there.
6. Where is she going to stay?	Sasha is going to stay at a fancy _____ near Central Park.
7. What is she going to see and do?	Sasha is going to visit the Statue of Liberty, _____, and the Empire State Building. She is going to see the _____ *Matilda*, and she is going to _____ and _____ in Central Park.

2 Read the sentences to start and end an email. Write the sentences in the correct column.

Please write back soon.   How are your parents?
Thanks for your email.   I got your email, thanks.
I hope you're well.   How are you?
What are you going to   When are you going to
do next summer?   go on vacation?

Start an email	End an email

REVIEW UNITS 9–10

1 Circle the correct answers.

Alice: I love ¹**winter / summer / fall** because it's hot and ²**snowy / sunny / icy**. It's the ³**most hot / more hot / hottest** season of the year. It's a good time to go ⁴**windsurfing / snowboarding / ice skating** and swimming.

Ben: I like ⁵**winter / spring / summer** because it's ⁶**cold / warm / hot** and sometimes snowy. It's a good time to go ⁷**snowboarding / windsurfing / swimming**, and skiing. It's the ⁸**colder / most cold / coldest** season of the year.

Tammy: I love ⁹**winter / spring / summer** because it is ¹⁰**icy / foggy / warm** and I can play baseball. I need my umbrella a lot because it's the ¹¹**foggiest / rainiest / most windy** season.

Pam: I love ¹²**spring / winter / fall** because the leaves are the ¹³**more colorful / most colorful / colorful** of any season. I think it's the ¹⁴**most pretty / prettiest / prettier** season of the year. It is cool outside. I can wear my ¹⁵**hoodie / shorts / T-shirt** playing basketball.

2 Write the names of the landforms.

| beach | jungle | mountains | river |
| hill | lake | ocean | |

1 _____ 2 _____
3 _____ 4 _____ 5 _____
6 _____ 7 _____

3 Match the questions with the correct answers.

1. Where is he going to go tomorrow?
2. Did he hike in the mountains yesterday?
3. When did he leave the beach yesterday?
4. What did he wear yesterday?
5. Are Brent and Ted going to wrestle tomorrow?
6. How many points did she get?

a. No, he didn't.
b. Shorts and a T-shirt.
c. To the desert.
d. Yes, they are.
e. Ten.
f. At noon.

4 Choose the correct answers.

1. A: _____ did Karen visit yesterday?
   a. Who   b. How   c. When
   B: She _____ her mom.
   a. is going to visit   b. visited   c. visits

2. A: Is Tim _____ to the beach today?
   a. going to go   b. went   c. will go
   B: No, he _____.
   a. isn't   b. didn't   c. doesn't

3. A: _____ you see your friends yesterday?
   a. Do   b. Did   c. Does
   B: Yes, I _____.
   a. do   b. didn't   c. did

4. A: Are they _____ later today?
   a. going to study   b. studied   c. studies
   B: No, they _____.
   a. aren't   b. didn't   c. don't

5. A: _____ did you cycle last weekend?
   a. Where   b. When   c. Why
   B: I _____ to the beach.
   a. cycled   b. am going to cycle   c. cycling

6. A: Where is Tim _____ on his vacation next week?
   a. go   b. going to go   c. went
   B: He _____ to the mountains.
   a. is going to go   b. are going   c. goes

70 | Review 5

5 Write yes/no questions and answers with be going to or the simple past.

1. Tom / play soccer / yesterday (no, basketball)
   Q: _Did Tom play soccer yesterday?_
   A: _No, he played basketball._

2. Tom and Mack / bowling / tomorrow? (yes)
   Q: _____
   A: _____

3. Jim / surfing / last summer? (no, snorkeling)
   Q: _____
   A: _____

4. You / swimming / next Saturday? (no, cycling)
   Q: _____
   A: _____

5. You / to Spain / last year (yes)
   Q: _____
   A: _____

6 Rewrite the sentences to make them correct.

1. Why don't we visiting the Tokyo?
   _____

2. What about go to the forest instead?
   _____

3. Jerry go to the sports event at June 2013.
   _____

4. We go swimming every day last summer.
   _____

5. I like summer because it is the hotter season.
   _____

6. Fall is the more beautiful season of the year.
   _____

7 Complete the conversations. Some of the words and phrases will be used more than once.

amazing	Let's	What did
cool	Really	Why don't
How was	What about	

1. A: _____ wear our new hoodies to play basketball.
   B: _____ we wear our sports jackets instead?

2. A: _____ go to Canada on vacation.
   B: It's too cold there in winter. _____ go to Hawaii.

3. A: _____ you do during your vacation?
   B: We went skydiving. It was _____!

4. A: _____ go skiing at Mount Kemo.
   B: _____? Isn't that too far away?

5. A: _____ your trip to Mexico last month?
   B: It was so _____!

6. A: _____ we travel to Europe?
   B: It's too far. _____ going to California instead?

8 Read the paragraph. Decide whether the sentences are true (T) or false (F).

Calvin likes to go running outside in the cold winter months. He wears his warmest tracksuit. As the winter season turns to spring and the weather is not as cold, Calvin likes to play tennis. He plays tennis in shorts and his hoodie. In the warm summer months, Calvin goes skateboarding a lot. He wears shorts, a T-shirt, and a baseball cap. Calvin plays soccer in the fall. He wears shorts and his favorite soccer shirt. On colder fall days, he wears a sweatshirt over his shirt.

1. Calvin likes to run in the winter. __T__
2. Calvin likes to play baseball in the spring. _____
3. He plays tennis in shorts and a hoodie. _____
4. Calvin wears a baseball cap to go skateboarding. _____
5. Calvin plays soccer in the summer. _____
6. Calvin wears a tracksuit to play soccer. _____

Fishing IN JAPAN

Unit 6 Video 6.1

BEFORE YOU WATCH

1 Look at the pictures from the video. Complete the sentences with the correct words.

| to catch | a fisherman | an island | tuna |

1. _____ is a very big fish.
2. _____ works on a boat.
3. _____ has water on all sides.
4. A fisherman's job is _____ fish.

WHILE YOU WATCH

2 Watch the video. Check [✔] the sentences you hear.

1. This is Japan, a country with thousands of islands. _____
2. These women are very young. _____
3. Fish is really good for you. _____
4. It's also difficult to catch! _____
5. The tuna is really happy. _____

3 Watch the video again. Circle the correct answers.

1. One-fifth of Japanese people are more than _____ years old.
   a. 55   b. 65   c. 75
2. The women find healthy _____ in the ocean.
   a. exercise   b. food   c. vegetables
3. Tuna is a very _____ fish in Japan.
   a. active   b. dangerous   c. popular
4. Osamu is very _____.
   a. fast   b. strong   c. tired

AFTER YOU WATCH

4 Complete the chart with your own information. Discuss: How often do you eat these foods?

Food	Once a week	Often (2–6 times a week)	Every day	Never
Vegetables			✗	
Rice / Pasta / Bread			✗	
Fish	✗			
Meat		✗		
Dessert				✗

> I eat vegetables and rice every day. I often eat fruit and meat. I eat fish once a week. I never eat dessert!

Dabbawallas

Unit 6 Video 6.3

BEFORE YOU WATCH

1 Look at the pictures from the video. Match them with the correct words.

dabbawalla   lunchbox   Mumbai   traffic

1.  _____   2.  _____   3.  _____   4. _____

2 Complete the sentences with the words from Exercise 1.

1. _____ is a big city in India.
2. Big cities always have a lot of _____.
3. A _____ takes lunch to people in India.
4. People put food for lunch in a _____.

WHILE YOU WATCH

3 Watch the video. When do you see these things? Write numbers 1 to 5.

1. _____ A man on a bicycle
2. _____ A man in a kitchen
3. _____ A map of Mumbai
4. _____ A man in an office building
5. _____ A lunchbox with rice

4 Watch the video again. Circle the correct answers.

1. The girl's **brother / cousin** works in Mumbai.
2. He takes **lunch / breakfast** to people.
3. A lot of people in India like **hot / cold** food for lunch.
4. There are about **4,000 / 40,000** dabbawallas in the city.
5. The job is **easy / dangerous**.

AFTER YOU WATCH

5 Work with a partner. Take turns asking and answering the questions.

Where do you eat lunch?

What do you usually eat?

Who makes your food?

What is your favorite lunch?

> I usually eat lunch in the cafeteria at my school.

Shark ATTACK!

Unit 7 Video 7.1

BEFORE YOU WATCH

1 Look at the pictures from the video. Match the words with the definitions.

a. shark

b. submarine

c. bite

1. to cut with your teeth _____

2. an underwater boat _____

3. a fish with very sharp teeth _____

WHILE YOU WATCH

2 Watch the video. When do you see these things? Write numbers 1 to 4.

_____ A shark biting a man

_____ A submarine going into the ocean

_____ A Greenland shark

_____ A Hammerhead shark

3 Watch the video again. Answer the questions about the Greenland shark.

1. In what ocean do the Greenland sharks live? _____

2. About how long can they be? _____

3. What kind of water do they like? _____

4. How deep can they go in the ocean? _____

5. How well do they see? _____

6. What kind of teeth do they have? _____

AFTER YOU WATCH

4 Work in small groups. Take turns describing different animals and guessing the names of the animals.

> It is usually green. It lives in water. It can jump.

> Is it a frog?

84 | Unit 7

Animals IN THE CITY!

Unit 7 Video 7.3

BEFORE YOU WATCH

1 Look at the pictures from the video. Match them with the correct words.

camel   cow   elephant   horse   monkey   snake

1. _____
2. _____
3. _____
4. _____
5. _____
6. _____

WHILE YOU WATCH

2 Watch the video. Circle the correct words.

1. There are a lot of **cats / rats** in the temple.
2. The rats eat **bananas / nuts**.
3. The rats drink **water / milk**.
4. In India, people think rats are **dangerous / special**.
5. People often **feed / eat** snakes in India.
6. At the end of the video, we see two men with two **snakes / elephants**.

3 Watch the video again. Are the sentences true (*T*) or false (*F*)? Correct the false sentences.

1. _____ More than a billion people live in India. _____
2. _____ There are more than 500 types of wild animals in this country. _____
3. _____ You can see camels and elephants in cities in India. _____
4. _____ People give milk with a little bit of honey to the rats. _____
5. _____ There is a camel festival in the town. _____

AFTER YOU WATCH

4 Work in small groups. Discuss: What animals live in cities in your country? Who takes care of these animals?

> A lot of people have dogs in their homes. People take care of their pets.

Rome: ANCIENT AND MODERN

Unit 8 Video 8.1

BEFORE YOU WATCH

1 Match the words with the definitions.

1. ancient _____
2. amphitheater _____
3. museum _____
4. modern _____

a. from the present
b. a place to see art and learn about history
c. from a long time ago
d. a place for games in ancient Rome

WHILE YOU WATCH

2 Watch the video. Are the sentences true (T) or false (F)? Correct the false sentences.

1. _____ There were theaters and markets and restaurants in ancient Rome. _____

2. _____ Sometimes people died in the fights in the Colosseum. _____

3. _____ People watch sports in the Colosseum today. _____

4. _____ Many modern stadiums are similar to the Colosseum. _____

3 Watch the video again. Circle the correct answers.

1. More than **3 million / 2 million** people visit Rome every year.
2. Even **3,000 / 2,000** years ago Rome was an important city.
3. About **1 million / 2 million** people lived in ancient Rome.
4. There were sometimes **1,000 / 10,000** people in the baths of ancient Rome at the same time.
5. There were about **50,000 / 5,000** people in the Colosseum in ancient Rome for every fight.

AFTER YOU WATCH

4 Work with a partner. Talk about a city near you. What can you do there? Where do you do it?

Where can I ride a bike?

You can go to the park.

86 | Unit 8

Crossing CITIES

Unit 8 Video 8.3

BEFORE YOU WATCH

1 Look at the pictures from the video. Match the kinds of transportation with the pictures.

1. _____

2. _____

3. _____

4. _____

a. Bullet Train   c. rickshaws
b. airplane   d. bus

WHILE YOU WATCH

2 Watch the video. Answer the questions with the correct words.

| Beijing | India | Japan | Mumbai | Tokyo |

1. What is the first city you see? _____
2. What country has rickshaws? _____
3. What city has cows in the streets? _____
4. What country is famous for its bullet trains? _____
5. In what city do a lot of people take planes to get to work? _____

3 Watch the video again. Circle the correct answers.

1. More than **20 million / 22 million** people live in Beijing.
2. There are about **50 million / 5 million** cars in Beijing.
3. People usually travel long distances by **train / bus** in Mumbai.
4. **Beijing / Tokyo** is the largest city in the world.
5. The Bullet Train travels at **300 / 330** kilometers per hour.

AFTER YOU WATCH

4 Work in small groups. Discuss: Where do you go on weekdays? On weekends? How do you travel? How long does it take?

> I usually take the bus to school. It takes about 20 minutes.

Unit 8 | 87

The PALIO

Unit 9 Video 9.1

BEFORE YOU WATCH

1 Complete the sentences with the correct words.

> Siena   Palio   horse   years

1. The _____ is a very special event.
2. _____ is a city in the north of Italy.
3. It started about 700 _____ ago, in the Middle Ages.
4. Ten riders from ten different areas of the city compete in the _____ race.

WHILE YOU WATCH

2 Watch the video. Complete the paragraph with the correct words.

> On the day of the race, there was a big parade. A lot of people
> ¹_____, the tradition of the Palio together.
> People ²_____ up in clothes from the Middle
> Ages and ³_____ traditional music. The parade
> ⁴_____ at the track in Siena's central square.
> Everybody was excited. We ⁵_____ for the race
> to begin.

3 Watch the video again. Answer the questions.

1. How often did Alberto practice for the race?
   _____

2. How long is the race?
   _____

3. What terrible thing happened in the race?
   _____

4. What did people do at the end of the race?
   _____

AFTER YOU WATCH

4 Work with a partner. Take turns asking and answering questions about an exciting game or celebration.

When was it?   Who was in it?
Where was it?   What happened?

(I went to a professional basketball game. It was really exciting!)

(When was it?)

(Last month.)

The BOWLER

Unit 9 Video 9.3

BEFORE YOU WATCH

1 Look at the pictures from the video. Complete the sentences with the correct words.

batter    bat    bowler

cricket    sign language

These boys are playing ¹_____. In this game,
the ²_____ throws the ball and the ³_____
hits it with a ⁴_____. This man is deaf. He cannot hear.
He uses ⁵_____ to communicate.

WHILE YOU WATCH

2 Watch the video. Are the sentences true (*T*) or false (*F*)? Correct the false sentences.

1. _____ Fahimuddin is 22 years old. _____

2. _____ Fahimuddin wants to be a professional baseball player. _____

3. _____ He can throw the ball over 160 kilometers an hour. _____

4. _____ He played cricket with his seven brothers as a child. _____

5. _____ He can't see very well. _____

3 Watch the video again. Answer the questions.

1. When did cricket start? _____
2. Where did cricket start? _____
3. How does Fahimuddin communicate? _____
4. What does a bowler do? _____

AFTER YOU WATCH

4 Work with a partner. Who are two of your favorite professional athletes? Why?

> My favorite athlete is David Ortiz. He plays baseball. He's a very good batter.

Unit 9 | 89

City OF WATER

Unit 10 Video 10.1

BEFORE YOU WATCH

1 Look at the pictures from the video. Complete the sentences.

canals in Venice

a gondola on a foggy day

masks for Carnevale in Venice

1. Venice has many streets of water called _____.
2. This is a special boat called a _____.
3. It's often hard to see in Venice because it's _____.
4. _____ is a big festival in Venice.
5. People wear amazing _____ at the festival.

WHILE YOU WATCH

2 Watch the video. Circle the correct answers.

1. Every day **16,000 / 60,000** people visit this city of water.
2. Venice is a city of **118 / 180** islands.
3. There are **170 / 177** canals in Venice.
4. The first Carnevale in Venice was in **1062 / 1162**.
5. There are **500 / 5,000** people at one of the parties!

3 Watch the video again. Complete the sentences.

1. Venice is in the northwest of _____.
2. The city is a group of _____.
3. There are no _____ in Venice.
4. Venetian _____ are very narrow boats.
5. People celebrate Carnevale in month of _____.
6. People wear _____ over their faces.

AFTER YOU WATCH

4 Work in small groups. Discuss: What are some special events in your country? Do you dress up in costume for any celebrations or festivals?

> I love St. Patrick's Day! Every year, I dress up in green clothes and only eat green food. Sometimes, I paint my hair green, too!

90 | Unit 10

Alaska!

Unit 10 Video 10.3

BEFORE YOU WATCH

1 Look at the pictures from the video. Complete the sentences with the correct words.

glacier   parachute   kayak

1. A _____ is a piece of equipment for jumping out of airplanes.
2. A _____ is a huge mountain of snow and ice.
3. People often use a _____ to explore rivers and lakes.

WHILE YOU WATCH

2 Watch the video. Circle the correct answers.

1. Alaska is next to _____.
   a. the United States   b. Canada   c. New York
2. Alaska is the _____ state in the United States.
   a. warmest   b. biggest   c. driest
3. The man is going to parachute over _____.
   a. rivers   b. beaches   c. glaciers
4. He's also going to _____ down some rivers.
   a. kayak   b. parachute   c. ski
5. He's going to _____ at night.
   a. see the Northern Lights   b. ski down icy mountains   c. camp by a river

3 Watch the video again. When do you see these things? Write numbers 1 to 5.

_____ skiing

_____ parachuting

_____ camping

_____ the Northern Lights

_____ kayaking

AFTER YOU WATCH

4 Work with a partner. Plan a four-day vacation. Describe where you're going to stay, what you're going to do, and what the weather is going to be like. Share your plans with the class.

> We're going to go to New York. We're going to stay in a hotel in Times Square. We're going to visit the Empire State Building.

This page intentionally left blank.

Irregular verbs

Base Verb	Simple Past
be	was, were
become	became
break	broke
build	built
buy	bought
can	could
choose	chose
come	came
do	did
draw	drew
drink	drank
drive	drove
eat	ate
fall	fell
feel	felt
find	found
fly	flew
get	got
give	gave
go	went
hang	hung
have	had
hear	heard
hold	held

Base Verb	Simple Past
know	knew
leave	left
lose	lost
make	made
meet	met
pay	paid
read	read
ride	rode
run	ran
say	said
see	saw
sell	sold
send	sent
sit	sat
sleep	slept
speak	spoke
spend	spent
swim	swam
take	took
teach	taught
think	thought
understand	understood
wear	wore
win	won

Credits

The publishers are grateful to the following for permission to reproduce copyright photographs and material:

Cover: ©John Hyde/Alamy; Back Cover (B/G): Shutterstock Images/photosoft; p. 2-3 (B/R) Alamy/© Blend Images; p. 4 (L) Shutterstock Images/Exactostock; p. 4 (T) Shutterstock Images/pukach; p. 4 (CR) © Radius Images / Alamy; p. 4 (c) Shutterstock Images/Sabphoto; p. 4 (TR) Shutterstock Images/Alan Poulson Photography; p. 5 (CR) Shutterstock Images/Armin Staudt; p. 6 (B/G) Shutterstock Images/FredS; p. 6 (TC) Shutterstock Images/sixninepixels; p. 6 (TR) Shutterstock Images/Dundanim; p. 6 (CR) Shutterstock Images/IngridHS; p. 6 (CL) Shutterstock Images/Pinkcandy; p. 6 (CL) Shutterstock Images/Tom Saga; p. 6 (BL) Alamy/© Radius Images; p. 6 (BC) Shutterstock Images/xavier gallego morell; p. 6 (BL) Shutterstock Images/hxdbzxy; p. 6 (TL) Shutterstock Images/Tyler Olson; p. 7 (TR) Shutterstock Images/Pressmaster; p. 8 (BL) Shutterstock Images/Pressmaster; p. 8 (TL) Shutterstock Images/KonstantinChristian; p. 8 (BC) Shutterstock Images/Sittipong; p. 8 (BCR) Shutterstock Images/Ingvar Bjork; p. 8 (BCL) Shutterstock Images/Phant; p. 10 (B/G) Shutterstock Images/pisaphotography; p. 10 (TCL) Superstock/Ambient Images Inc. ; p. 10 (TL) Alamy/© TNT Magazine; p. 10 (B/G) Shutterstock Images/Songquan Deng; p. 10 (TR) Shutterstock Images/yanugkelid; p. 10 (TL) Shutterstock Images/igor.stevanovic; 10 (TCL) Alamy/© David Grossman; p. 11 (CL) Shutterstock Images/zirconicusso; p. 11 (TC) Shutterstock Images/ribeiroantonio; p. 11 (TL) Shutterstock Images/edel; p. 11 (BC) Shutterstock Images/ID1974; p. 12-13 (B/G) Shutterstock Images/Omegafoto; p. 12 (C) Shutterstock Images/Joana Lopes; p. 12 (inset) Image provided by the SeaWiFS Project; NASA/Goddard Space Flight Center; and ORBIMAGE; p. 13 (9) Shutterstock Images/Brian A Jackson; p. 13 (1): iStockphoto/AnthonyRosenberg; p. 13 (4): ©Richard Sharrocks / Alamy; p. 13 (6): ©graficart.net / Alamy; p. 13 (10): ©Andres Rodriguez / Alamy; p. 13 (11): ©Lusoimages - Technology / Alamy; p. 13 (12): ©music Alan King / Alamy; p. 13 (2) Shutterstock Images/artjazz; p. 13 (5R) LES BREAULT/©Alamy; p. 13 (5) Alamy/© LES BREAULT ; p. 13 (5) Alamy/©FILM STILLS; p. 13 (7) Shuttertstock Images/Denys Prykhodov; p. 13 (8) Alamy/©Nikreates; p. 14 (L): ©DEAN LEWINS/epa/Corbis; p. 14 (R): ©DANIEL MUNOZ/Reuters/Corbis; p. 16 (TL) Alamy/©Paul Paddison ; p. 17 (CR) Alamy/©RubberBall; p. 18 (BC) Shutterstock Images/Dan Thornberg; p. 18 (TL) Shutterstock Images/dotshock; p. 18 (BR) Shutterstock Images/Lightspring; p. 18 (BL) Shutterstock Images/Michael Rosskothen; p. 19 (TR) Shutterstock Images/pedalist; p. 20 (CR) Shutterstock Images/iQoncept; p. 20 (TR) Shutterstock Images/art-Tayga; p. 20 (CR) Shutterstock Images/Globe Turner; p. 20 (BC) Shutterstock Images/Manczurov; p. 20 (TR) Shutterstock Images/Stephen Firmender; p. 21 (TL) Shutterstock Images/cristovao; p. 21 (BL) Shutterstock Images/cristovao; p. 21 (C) Alamy/©David Young-Wolff; p. 22-23 (B/G) Shutterstock Images/Cora Mueller; p. 23 (L): ©Blend Images / Alamy; p. 23 (CL): Stock Connection / SuperStock; p. 23 (BL): Shutterstock/Angela Hawkey; p. 23 (BCL): Gareth Boden; p.23 (BC): ©imagebroker / Alamy; p. 23 (TR): Shutterstock/Jacek Chabraszewski; p. 23 (CR) Shutterstock Images/aastock; p. 23 (TCR) Shutterstock Images/Stuart Monk; p. 23 (BC) Alamy/©moodboard ; p. 23 (BCR) Shutterstock Images/Monkey Business Images; p. 23 (CR) Shutterstock Images/aastock; p. 23 (TCL) Shutterstock Images/photobank.ch; p. 23 (TCR) Shutterstock Images/racorn; p. 24 (B/G) Shutterstock Images/ffolas ; p. 24 (T): Photo Kevin Farmer / APN; p. 24 (BL): Photo Kevin Farmer / APN; p. 26 (B/G) © Kathleen Smith / Alamy; p. 26 (B/G) Alamy/©Kathleen Smith; p. 27 (R) Shutterstock Images/CREATISTA; p. 28 (BL) Shutterstock Images/Popartic; p. 28 (TL) Alamy/©PhotoAlto; p. 28 (CT): Shutterstock/CREATISTA; p. 28 (CB): Shutterstock/Photosindiacom, LLC; p. 28 (B): ©Young-Wolff Photography / Alamy; p. 29 (T): ©RubberBall / Alamy; p. 30 (TR): ©India Picture/Corbis; p. 30 (TL): Shutterstock/v.s.anandhakrishna; p. 30 (B/G) Shutterstock Images/Shyamalamuralinath; p. 31 (3) Shutterstock Images/milezaway; p. 31 (1) Shutterstock Images/Monkey Business Images; p. 31 (2) Shutterstock Images/Blend Images; p. 31 (5) Shutterstock Images/Ollyy; p. 31 (4) Shutterstock Images/Gina Smith; p. 31 (3) Alamy/©Stock Connection Distribution; p. 32-33 (c) © Mark A. Johnson/Corbis; p. 33 (i) Shutterstock Images/johnfoto18; p. 33 (b) Shutterstock Images/Kamira; p. 33 (a) Shutterstock Images/Maridav; p. 33 (BL) Superstock/Blend Images; p. 33 (j) Alamy/©Megapress; p. 33 (g) Alamy/©whiteboxmedia limited ; p. 33 (f) Shutterstock Images/philippou; p. 33 (e) Shutterstock Images/Africa Studio; p. 33 (d) Shutterstock Images/RoJo Images; p. 33 (c) Alamy/©Image Source; p. 34 (T) Shutterstock Images/Tracy Whiteside; p. 34 (BL) Alamy/©Megapress; p. 34 (C) Shutterstock Images/Tracy Whiteside; p. 34 (TL) Shutterstock Images/Olyina; p. 35 (CL) Shutterstock Images/Jorg Hackemann; p. 36 (g) Shutterstock Images/Anna Jurkovska; p. 36 (h) Shutterstock Images/Andrey Yurlov; p. 36 (f) Shutterstock Images/Zhukov Oleg; 36 (e) Shutterstock Images/Mike Flippo; p. 36 (d) Shutterstock Images/Be Good; p. 36 (c) Shutterstock Images/Rob Marmion; p. 36 (b) Shutterstock Images/Photosani; p. 36 (a) Shutterstock Images/dean bertoncelj; p. 36 (TL) Corbis/©68/Ocean; p. 37 (TR) Shutterstock Images/nakamasa; p. 38 (CL) Shutterstock Images/Jeka; p. 38 (BC) Shutterstock Images/Maria Maarbes; p. 39 (TL) Shutterstock Images/Max Topchii; p. 40 (TR) Shutterstock Images/Visun Khankasem; p. 40 (BC) Alamy/©epa european pressphoto agency b.v. ; p. 40 (CR) Superstock/age fotostock; p. 40 (CR) Alamy/©Richard Levine; p. 40 (B/G) Shutterstock Images/CHAINFOTO24; p. 42-43 (C) Corbis/©Hero Images; p. 43 (10) Shutterstock Images/Monkey Business Images; p. 43 (9) Shutterstock Images/hxdbzxy; p. 43 (8) Alamy/©B. Leighty/Photri Image; p. 43 (7) Alamy/©Art Directors & TRIP ; p. 43 (6) Shutterstock Images/Gina Smith; p. 43 (5) Alamy/©Blend Images ; p. 43 (4) Alamy/©apply pictures; p. 43 (3) Shutterstock Images/michaeljung; p. 43 (2) Alamy/©Janine Wiedel Photolibrary; p. 44 (BG): ©Chen Xiaodong/Xinhua Press/Corbis; p. 44 (C): ©F. Jack Jackson / Alamy; p. 45 (TR) Shutterstock Images/mekCar; p. 46 (TC) Alamy/©Jack Carey; p. 47 Alamy/©China Images ; p. 48 Shutterstock Images/BrianWancho; p. 49 Alamy/©Radius Images; p. 50 (B/G) Shutterstock Images/art_of_sun; p. 50 (B/G) Alamy/©Christina Kennedy; p. 50 (c) Alamy/©B.O'Kane; p. 50 (a) Alamy/©Stock Connection Blue; p. 50 (b) Alamy/©Blend Images; p. 51 (5) Shutterstock Images/Dancestrokes; p. 51 (6) Shutterstock Images/Pablo Hidalgo; p. 51 (2) Shutterstock Images/mrHanson; p. 51 (4) Shutterstock Images/Olinchuk; p. 51 (1) Alamy/©Michael Neelon; p. 52 (B/G): Stuart Westmorland/Image Source/Corbis; p. 54 Shutterstock Images/Gyorgy Barna ; p. 54-55 (B/G) Shutterstock Images/photka; p. 55 (12) Shutterstock Images/jantarus; p. 55 (11) Shutterstock Images/Olga Popova; p. 55 (10) Shutterstock Images/VladaKela; p. 55 (17) Shutterstock Images/fototip; p. 55 (13) Shutterstock Images/Gregory Gerber; p. 55 (14) Shutterstock Images/indigolotos; p. 55 (16) Shutterstock Images/Alex Studio; p. 55 (17) Shutterstock Images/Hurst Photo; p. 55 (15) Shutterstock Images/Naufal MQ; p. 55 (2) Shutterstock Images/KIM NGUYEN; p. 55 (9) Shutterstock Images/KIM NGUYEN; p. 55 (7) Shutterstock Images/Maks Narodenko; p. 55 (1) Shutterstock Images/Nagritsamon Ruksujjar; 55 (3) Shutterstock Images/Alex Studio; p. 55 (4) Shutterstock Images/EM Arts; p. 55 (5) Shutterstock Images/hannadarzy; 55 (6) Shutterstock Images/Michal Nowosielski; p. 55 (8) Shutterstock Images/Yakov Oskanov; p. 56 (TR): ©Manzo Niikura/amanaimages/Corbis; p. 56 (CL): ©MIXA / Alamy; p. 56 (CR): ©MIXA / Alamy; p. 56 (B/G) Shutterstock Images/JOAT; p. 56 (C) Shutterstock Images/Nataliya Arzamasova; p. 58 (j) Shutterstock Images/amphaiwan; p. 58 (c) Alamy/©amana images inc.. p. 58 (TL) Shutterstock Images/Diana Taliun; p. 58 (a) Alamy/©imageBROKER ; p. 58 (b) Shutterstock Images/Shebeko; p. 58 (e) Shutterstock Images/dotshock; p. 58 (k) Alamy/©whiteboxmedia limited ; p. 58 (i) Shutterstock Images/Active branding; p. 58 (f) Alamy/©Handmade Pictures ; p. 58 (h) Shutterstock Images/Hurst Photo; p. 59 (BR) Shutterstock Images/Sally Scott; p. 60 (TL) Alamy/©Image Source; p. 60 (BL) Shutterstock Images/Grounder; p. 60 (BL) Shutterstock Images/mahmuttibet; p. 61 (TR) Shutterstock Images/Petr Jilek; p. 62 (TR) courtesy of Dominic Lau/Don Chow Tacos; p. 62 (CL) courtesy of Dominic Lau/Don Chow Tacos; p. 62 (CR) courtesty of Virginia Ginsburg; p. 62 (B/G) Shutterstock Images/Annareichel; p. 62 (B/G) Shutterstock Images/giftzyx; p. 64-65 (B/G): Shutterstock/Sylvie Bouchard; p. 66 (TL): Fotosearch / SuperStock; p. 66 (CL): ©tbkmedia.de / Alamy; p. 66 (BL): ©Joe McDonald/Corbis; p. 66 (TR): Thomas Marent/Minden Pictures/FLPA; p. 66: (a) Shutterstock Images/Kletr; p. 66: (b) Shutterstock Images/Piotr Krzeslak; p. 66: (f) Glow Images/Jevgenija Pigozne/ImageBROKER; p. 66: (h) Shutterstock Images/Michiel de Wit; p. 67 (TR): Frans Lanting/FLPA; p. 67: (B/G) Shutterstock Images/Aleksandr Bryliaev; p. 68: (T) Alamy/©frans lemmens; p. 68: (1) Shutterstock Images/Jeff Dalton; p. 68: (2) Shutterstock Images/Shane Myers Photography; p. 68: (3) Alamy/©Juniors Bildarchiv GmbH; p. 68: (4) SuperStock/Biosphoto; p. 68: (5) SuperStock/NHPA; p.68: (6) Masterfile/Minden Pictures; p. 68: (7) SuperStock/©Frank Sommariva/image/imagebroker.net; p. 69 (TR): ©i love images / women's lifestyle / Alamy; p. 70 (B/G) Shutterstock Images/Abigail210986; p. 70: (TL) Alamy/©Kumar Sriskandan; p.70: (TR) Shutterstock Images/stevemart; p. 70: (BL) Shutterstock Images/ntstudio; p. 71 (TR): ©Arletta Cwalina / Alamy; p. 72: (TL) Shutterstock Images/mariait; p. 72 (TR): Getty Images/Wayne R Bilenduke; p. 72 (BC); imagebroker.net / SuperStock; p. 74-75: (B/G) Getty Images/Martin Puddy; p. 75 (a): ©OJO Images Ltd / Alamy; p. 75 (b): ©Radius Images / Alamy; p. 75 (c): ©Andrew Fox / Alamy; p. 75 (d): ©Randy Faris/Corbis; p. 75 (f): Tony Garcia / SuperStock; p. 75 (g): ©Bubbles Photolibrary / Alamy; p. 75: (e) SuperStock/©Flirt; p. 75: (h) Alamy/©El Chapulin; p. 75: (i) SuperStock/©Allindiaimages; p. 75: (j) Masterfile/andresr/Crestock; p. 76 (T): ©Ammit / Alamy; p. 76 (B): Tony Waltham/Robert Harding; p. 76 (CL): ©Robert Harding Picture Library Ltd / Alamy; p. 76 (CL): Peter Barritt / Robert Harding Picture Library / SuperStock; p. 77: (CR) Media Bakery/Matz Sjöberg; p. 78: (T) Alamy/© D. Hurst; p. 78: (a) Alamy/©Peter Horree; p. 78: (b) Alamy/©Caro; p. 78: (c) Shutterstock Images/Andrey Khrolenok; p. 78: (d) Alamy/©LOOK Die Bildagentur der Fotografen GmbH; p. 78: (e) Shutterstock Images/Dabarti CGI; p. 78: (f) Alamy/©Richard Levine; p. 78: (g) Alamy/©Don Klumpp; p. 78: (h) Shutterstock Images/guroldinneden; p. 79: (BR) Alamy/©Kumar Sriskandan; p. 80: (T) Masterfile/David Zimmerman; p. 80: (2) Shutterstock Images/CristinaMuraca; p. 80: (3) Shutterstock Images/Oleksiy Mark; p. 80: (BL) Shutterstock Images/Leanne Vorrias; p. 81: (TR) Shutterstock Images/Alberto Loyo; p. 82: (B/G) Shutterstock Images/gyn9037; p. 82: (1) age fotostock/© Fumio; p. 82 (CT): ©DBURKE / Alamy; p. 82 (CL): ©Tetra Images / Alamy; p. 82 (CB): ©dbimages / Alamy; p. 82 (CB): ©UrbanEye / Alamy; p. 84-85 (B/G): ©Aurora Photos / Alamy; p. 85: (1) Shutterstock Images/StacieStauffSmith Photos; p. 85 (2): Shutterstock/gorillaimages; p. 85 (3): Shutterstock/Tom Gowanlock; p. 85 (5): ©Aflo Foto Agency / Alamy; p. 85 (7): ©Shaun Wilkinson / Alamy; p. 85 (10): Getty Images/Happy to share the beauty I see in my travels; p. 85 (11): Thinkstock; p. 85: (4) Shutterstock Images/pio3; p. 85: (6) Alamy/©Andres Rodriguez; p. 85: (8) Shutterstock Images/EcoPrint; p. 85: (9) Shutterstock Images/Andrey_Popov; p. 86 (TL): ©Bernard Bisson/Sygma/Corbis; p. 87: (TR) SuperStock/©Exactostock; p. 88: (T) Shutterstock Images/Marco Prati; p. 88: (a) Shutterstock Images/mimon!; p. 88: (b) Shutterstock Images/Alexander Kalina; p. 88: (c) Shutterstock Images/Neveshkin Nikolay; p. 88: (d) Shutterstock Images/Vlue; p. 88: (e) Shutterstock Images/Elnur; p. 88: (f) Shutterstock Images/Karkas; p. 88: (g) Alamy/©D. Hurst; p. 88: (h) Shutterstock Images/Elnur; p. 88: (i) Shutterstock Images/Petar Djordjevic; p. 88: (j) Shutterstock Images/Vlue; p. 88: (k) Shutterstock Images/In Green; p. 88: (L) Shutterstock Images/Karkas; p. 89: (CR) Shutterstock Images/Maxim Blinkov; p. 90: (T) Shutterstock Images/Pistryy Valeriy; p. 90: (2) Shutterstock Images/Pavel L Photo and Video; p. 90: (3) Shutterstock Images/pryzmat; p. 90: (4) Alamy/©Extreme Sports Photo; p. 91: (T) Alamy/©epa european pressphoto agency b.v.; p. 92: (bkgd t) Alamy/©dbimages; p. 92: (TR) Shutterstock Images/James Steidl; p. 94-95 (B/G): Panos/Fredrik Naumann; p. 95: (8) Alamy/©PhotoStock-Israel; p. 96: (a) Alamy/©Westend61 GmbH; p. 95 (1): ©Angie Sharp / Alamy; p. 95 (2): PETER SKINNER/SCIENCE PHOTO LIBRARY; p. 95 (3): ©Juniors Bildarchiv GmbH / Alamy; p. 95 (4): London News Pictures/Rex Features; p. 95 (5): ©Fredrick Kippe / Alamy; p. 95 (6): ©Design Pics Inc. / Alamy; p. 95 (7): ©Radius Images/Corbis; p. 95 (B): ©Gay Bumgarner / Alamy; p. 96: (b) Alamy/©Gary Dublanko; p. 96: (c) Alamy/©i travel; p. 97: (T) Shutterstock Images/monticello; p. 98: (T) Alamy/©Robert Fried; p. 98: (2) Shutterstock Images/Vlada Z; p. 98 (6): ©travelbild.com / Alamy; p. 98: (3) Shutterstock Images/David Krijgsman; p. 98: (4) Shutterstock Images/Matt Tilghman; p. 98: (5) Shutterstock Images/Meg007; p. 98: (BL) Shutterstock Images/Steve Whiston; p. 99: (TR) Shutterstock Images/EllenSmile; p. 99: (BR) Shutterstock Images/Arsgera; p. 100: (TL) SuperStock/©Cusp; p. 100: (BL) Shutterstock Images/Chaikovskiy Igor; p. 101: (TR) Newscom/Bettina Strenske imageBROKER; p. 102: (B/G) Shutterstock Images/Krishna.Wu; p. 102: (TL) Shutterstock Images/Marques; p. 102 (TL): ©Egmont Strigl / Alamy; p. 102 (CL): Shutterstock/B Calkins; p. 102 (BL): ©Richard Hamilton Smith/CORBIS; p.102 (TR): Bill Coster/FLPA; p. 102 (CR): ©Oleksiy Maksymenko/All Canada Photos/Corbis; p. 102 (CR): ©Free Agents Limited/CORBIS; p. 102 (BR): ©CBW / Alamy; p. 104-105: (B/G) SuperStock/©Dave Fleetham/Pacific Stock - Design Pics; p. 117 (TC) Shutterstock Images/Mike Peters; p. 117 (CR) Shutterstock Images/Edith60; p. 117 (CL) Shutterstock Images/Dominique de La Croix; p. 119: (1) Alamy/©Joshua Dale Rablin; p. 119: (2) Shutterstock Images/Stayer; p. 119: (3) Shutterstock Images/Mr. SUTTIPON YAKHAM; p. 119: (4) Shutterstock Images/Audrey Snider-Bell; p. 120: (TR) Alamy/©Peter Barritt; p. 120: (CR) Shutterstock Images/clivewa

The publishers are grateful to the following illustrators:

David Belmonte (Beehive Illustration) p. 26, 27
Anni Betts pp. 52, 53, 104, 105
Nigel Dobbyn (Beehive Illustration) p. 119
Ian Escott (Beehive Illustration) p. 73
Q2A Media Services, Inc. p. 3, 16, 34, 46, 59, 70, 78, 83, 117, 118
Jose Rubio p. 57, 63
Sean Tiffany p. 4, 8, 44, 67, 69.

All video stills by kind permission of:

Discovery Communications, LLC 2015: p. 2 (1,3), 8, 10, 12 (1, 3, 4), 15, 20, 21, 22 (1, 3, 4), 25, 30, 32 (1, 3, 4, 35, 38, 40, 41, 42 (1, 3), 45, 51, 54 (1, 3, 4), 57, 62, 63, 64 (1, 3, 4), 67, 72, 73, 74 (1, 3, 4), 77, 82, 84 (1, 3), 87, 92, 94 (1, 3, 4), 97, 103. 116, 117, 118, 119, 120

Cambridge University Press: p. 2 (2), 8, 12 (2), 18, 22 (2), 28, 32 (2), 42 (2), 48, 54 (2), 60, 64 (2), 70, 74 (2), 80, 84 (2), 90, 94 (2), 100

Credits

Photo Credits:

Cover: ©John Hyde/Alamy; Back Cover (B/G): Shutterstock Images/photosoft; p. 10 (TL): REX/Startraks Photo; p. 10 (TR): Tony Gonzalez/Everett Collection/Alamy; p. 10 (CL): Featureflash/Shutterstock; p. 10 (CR): Dfree/Shutterstock; p. 10 (BL): REX/Startraks Photo; p 10 (BR): Everett Collection/Shutterstock; p. 11 (TL): Image Source/SuperStock; p. 11 (BR): Datacraft - Sozaijiten/Alamy; p. 17 (TL): ©Richard Sharrocks / Alamy; p. 17 (TR): iStockphoto/AnthonyRosenberg; p. 17 (CL): ©Art Directors & TRIP / Alamy; p. 17 (CR): ©Caro / Alamy; p. 17 (BL): ©music Alan King / Alamy; p. 17 (BR): ©graficart.net / Alamy; p. 21 (T): Featureflash/Shutterstock; p. 23: Getty/Adrianna Williams/The Image Bank; p. 30 (1): Alamy/Archimage; p. 30 (2): Alamy/Janine Wiedel Photolibrary; p. 30 (3): Alamy/Andrew Fox; p. 30 (4): Alamy/Mike Booth; p. 30 (5): Alamy/Archimage; p. 30 (6): Alamy/redsnapper; p. 30 (7): Alamy/Peter Titmuss; p. 30 (8): Shutterstock/Monkey Business Images; p. 30 (9): Alamy/Janine Wiedel Photolibrary; p. 30 (10): Alamy/VIEW Pictures Ltd.; p. 36 (a): Shutterstock/Larina Natalia; p. 36 (b): Alamy/Richard Levine; p. 36 (c): KIM NGUYEN/Shutterstock; p. 36 (d): Shutterstock/Lasse Kristensen; p. 36 (e): Shutterstock/MaraZe; p. 36 (f): Olga Popova/Shutterstock; p. 36 (g): Alamy/John James; p. 36 (h): Shutterstock/Robyn Mackenzie; p. 36 (i): jantarus/Shutterstock; p. 37 (L): Alamy/Hera Food; p. 37 (R): Shutterstock/foodiepics; p. 40 (L): Shutterstock/zirconicusso; p. 40 (T): Shutterstock/Studiotouch; p. 40 (B): Shutterstock/highviews; p. 45 (1): Alamy/Sarah Peters/imagebroker; p. 45 (2): Getty/ranplett/Vetta; p. 45 (3): Superstock/Science Photo Library; p. 45 (4): Alamy/kpzfoto; p. 45 (5): Shutterstock/andamanec; p. 45 (6): Superstock/Tips Images; p. 45 (TR): Blend Images/Shutterstock; p. 46 (TL): Alamy/©Juniors Bildarchiv GmbH; p. 46 (TCL): Shutterstock Images/Shane Myers Photography; p. 46 (BCL): SuperStock/NHPA; p. 46 (BL): SuperStock/©Frank Sommariva/image/ imagebroker.net; p. 46 (TR): Shutterstock Images/Jeff Dalton; p. 46 (CR): SuperStock/Biosphoto; p. 46 (BR): Masterfile/Minden Pictures; p. 47 (L):Alamy/Dallas and John Heaton/Travel Pictures; p. 47 (C): Alamy/David Cantrille; p. 47 (R): Getty/David Wall Photo/Lonely Planet Images; p. 49 (TR): Vladimir Melnik/Shutterstock; p. 49 (CR): MartinMaritz/Shutterstock; p. 50 (a): fiphoto/Shutterstock; p. 50 (b): Getty/Atlantide S.N.C./age fotostock; p. 50 (c): Alamy/PBimages; p. 50 (d): ValeStock/Shutterstock; p. 50 (e): Alamy/Marc Macdonald; p. 50 (f): Alamy/eye35.pix; p. 50 (g): Alamy/Aardvark; p. 50 (h): Shutterstock/Tischenko Irina; p. 50 (i): Alamy/Stephen Dorey ABIPP; p. 50 (j): Alamy/incamerastock; p. 55 (TR): Rob Marmion/Shutterstock; p. 56 (a): ChameleonsEye/Shutterstock; p. 56 (b): Paul Banton/Shutterstock; p. 56 (c): Ulrich Mueller/Shutterstock; p. 56 (d): Walter Bibikow/Mauritius/SuperStock; p. 56 (e): Glow Images/SuperStock; p. 56 (f): Robert Kneschke/Shutterstock; p. 56 (g): nodff/Shutterstock; p. 56 (h): FloridaStock/Shutterstock; p. 56 (i): Smereka/Shutterstock; p. 56 (j): Franck Boston/Shutterstock; p. 58 (T1): Ipatov/Shutterstock; p. 58 (T2): Getty/technotr/E+; p. 58 (T4): Shutterstock/oliveromg; p. 58 (T5): Shutterstock/Jacek Chabraszewski; p. 58 (T7): tammykayphoto/Shutterstock; p. 58 (T9): Tony Garcia / SuperStock; p. 58 (B2): Shutterstock/Petrenko Andriy; p. 58 (B3): Alamy/PictureNet Corporation; p. 58 (B6): Corbis/Chris Cole/Duomo; p. 58 (B8): Pistryy Valeriy/Shutterstock; p. 58 (B10): Getty/Mike Kemp; p. 58 (B11): Shutterstock/YanLev; p. 63 (T): lev radin/Shutterstock

The publishers are grateful to the following illustrators:

Janet Allinger p. 6, 20, 34, 54, 68; David Belmonte (Beehive Illustration) p. 3, 4, 26, 38, 59, 60, 61; Anni Betts p. 13, 22, 67, 70, 75; Galia Bernstein (NB Illustration) p. 17,19, 51; Alberto de Hoyos p. 53; Nigel Dobbyn (Beehive Illustration) p. 33, 40, 41, 48, 79; Q2A Media Services, Inc. p. 2, 7, 8, 32, 48, 52; Jose Rubio p. 2, 14, 16, 31, 39, 42, 43, 64, 65, 66, 69; David Shephard (Bright Agency) p. 24, 26, 44; Sean Tiffany p. 9, 11, 18, 25, 29, 40, 46, 62, 70, 71, 80; Laszlo Veres (Beehive Illustration) p. 68.

Video Stills:

Discovery Communications, LLC 2015: pages 72, 73, 74, 76, 77, 78, 81, 82, 83, 84, 85, 86, 87, 88, 89, 90, & 91.

Notes

Notes

Notes